SpringerBriefs in Computer Science

Series Editors
Stan Zdonik
Peng Ning
Shashi Shekhar
Jonathan Katz
Xindong Wu
Lakhmi C. Jain
David Padua
Xuemin (Sherman) Shen
Borko Furht
V.S. Subrahmanian
Martial Hebert
Katsushi Ikeuchi
Bruno Siciliano

For further volumes:
http://www.springer.com/series/10028

Vishnu Nath • Stephen E. Levinson

Autonomous Robotics and Deep Learning

Springer

Vishnu Nath
Seattle, WA, USA

Stephen E. Levinson
University of Illinois at Urbana-Champaign
Urbana, IL, USA

ISSN 2191-5768   ISSN 2191-5776 (electronic)
ISBN 978-3-319-05602-9 ISBN 978-3-319-05603-6 (eBook)
DOI 10.1007/978-3-319-05603-6
Springer Cham Heidelberg New York Dordrecht London

Library of Congress Control Number: 2014935166

Printed on acid-free paper

Springer is part of Springer Science+Business Media (www.springer.com)

*To my parents, Kamal and Jaya, to whom
I owe all my achievements*

*To my advisor, Dr. Levinson, for all his
help and advice*

*To my lab partners, Aaron and Luke,
for all their help and support*

To my alma mater

Contents

Chapter 1
Introduction

Almost all of us have watched plenty of sci-fi movies that revolve around the same theme: scientists develop a robot that has true consciousness, observes the environment around it and realizes that human beings are an unnecessary part of the equation. Half an hour into the movie and we have an army of intelligent robots that are hell-bent on destroying the human civilization and the protagonist manages to explode a central server or insert a virus into it, deactivating all the robots and saving our civilization. In spite of all this, most of us would like robots to perform various day-to-day activities that we hate doing, freeing up our time for activities that we enjoy a lot more. The commercial success of Roomba is proof that consumers are willing to pay for personal assistants and more importantly, that they do not have a deep mistrust for robots. Perhaps the form factor of a Roomba might be crucial for people to think that in case of a robot uprising, there isn't much to worry about from a Roomba!

Hearing the word "robot" instantly brings images of ferocious metal creatures that possess some of the most dangerous weapons known to us. To encapsulate, Hollywood isn't exactly the best PR agent for the field of robotics! Technically speaking, there is no particular form factor for a robot. It can be any shape and size, and can possess a variety of tools or just a single tool, based on its intended function (Spong et al. 2006). For instance, most people will agree that a robotic arm with a three-pronged claw that moves boxes from one point to another is a robot. It just seems right because it tallies with what we consider to be the image of a quintessential industrial robot. However, would you consider a conveyor belt as a robot? It too performs the task of moving an object from one place to another, and is also controlled by electronic control systems and computers. The truth is that the term "robot" is actually very broad and encompasses a lot of beautifully designed machines.

Another field that is very closely related to the field of robotics is the field of artificial intelligence. So closely related are the two fields that the general population considers one term to imply the other. Broadly speaking, artificial intelligence is the study and design of agents that seem to behave in an intelligent manner (Russell and Norvig 2010). The agent can be virtual or physical, and by intelligent

V. Nath and S.E. Levinson, *Autonomous Robotics and Deep Learning*, SpringerBriefs in Computer Science, DOI 10.1007/978-3-319-05603-6_1, © The Author(s) 2014

behavior we mean the ability to perceive its immediate surroundings and maximize its utility and odds of survival. Maximizing the odds of survival is the primordial instinct of all life forms and the ability to detect threats and take appropriate action is a measure of intelligence. As a simpler way of understanding, consider the field of robotics to deal with the human body while the field of artificial intelligence to deal with the human mind. They are both separate entities but each requires the other to be able to do anything. Artificial intelligence deals with algorithms that have inputs and outputs. If these inputs are from the physical realm, robots have transducers to convert the physical stimuli into a form that can be understood by the AI algorithms, and convert the output from the AI algorithms to have a physical impact on the environment. As a result, AI algorithms are highly modular and versatile, they can work across a wide variety of scenarios.

The field of artificial intelligence is divided into two camps—strong AI and weak AI. The camp of weak AI say that the field of artificial intelligence will only be able to produce agents that seem to behave intelligently. These agents would forever be simply following the algorithm and have no understanding of what they are doing, and will operate in a non-terminating loop. Advocates of the strong AI camp say that artificial intelligence would be able to do everything that weak AI can do and develop consciousness. They advocate that the AI agents will be self-aware and aware of their surroundings and will be able to "think" just like humans do (Russell and Norvig 2010). The vast majority of practical applications that AI is able to perform today comes under the domain of the weak AI camp. These are specific applications that the agent is programmed to do and it performs the best possible action based on the information available at the time. Strong AI is a research subject with thousands of computer scientists working in the hope of being able to create a mind or develop consciousness for a non-living entity. However, the possibility and negative ramifications of strong AI is a favorite for all the science fiction writers (refer to near apocalypse scenario at the beginning of this chapter!) (Asimov 2008). The closest we have to strong AI is the development of a sub-category of artificial intelligence called Machine Learning.

Machine learning attempts to "learn" from available date. The available data is given as training data and the machine learning algorithm forms a representation on this basis. Once the training is completed, a new unseen data point is presented to the algorithm and it should be able to classify this point, with reasonable accuracy and confidence, based on previous data. A common example of such a system in our day-to-day lives is the email spam detector. The way the detector works is by providing it a bunch of spam emails that have been explicitly labeled as spam. Also, provide it with a bunch of regular emails that have been labeled as non-spam. Now, when a new email arrives, the detector is able to classify it as spam or non-spam (Michalski and Mitchell 1983). Of course, even the best of these systems make mistakes and are in a state of constant improvisation.

In this book, we make an attempt to bridge the gap between weak AI and strong AI through the use of a robotic platform. We programmed a humanoid robot to be able to solve a 3D maze using a ball as a visual indicator. The only thing that was pre-programmed was to look for the start and end points of the maze.

The robot would have to determine the shortest path between the two points, if it existed, and rotate the board on which the maze was built so that the ball can roll over to the intended spot. Multiple iterations had to be performed over various maze layouts so that the robot can understand its goal and the actions that are available to it to achieve the goal. Of tremendous importance is the fact that the robot can realize its actions have an influence on the environment, a small step in the direction of strong AI. The various components of the entire system that have made this project a reality are discussed in subsequent chapters of this book.

References

Asimov, I. (2008). *I, Robot*. Spectra.

Breazeal, C., Wang, A., & Picard, R. (2007). Experiments with a Robotic Computer: Body, Affect and Cognition Interactions. *HRI'07* (pp. 153–160). Arlington, Virginia: ACM.

Kormushev, P., Calinon, S., Saegusa, R., & Metta, G. (2010). Learning the skill of archery by a humanoid iCub. *2010 IEEE-RAS International Conference on Humanoid Robotics*. Nashville.

Metta, G., Sandini, G., Vernon, D., & Natale, L. (2008). The iCub humanoid robot: an open platform for research in embodied cognition. *8th Workshop on performance metrics for intelligent systems*. ACM.

Michalski, R., Carbonell J., & Mitchell, T. (1983). *Machine Learning*. Palo Alto: Tioga Publishing Company.

Michie, D. (1986). *On Machine Intelligence*. New York: John Wiley & Sons.

Nath, V., & Levinson, S. (2013a). Learning to Fire at Targets by an iCub Humanoid Robot. *AAAI Spring Symposium*. Palo Alto: AAAI.

Nath, V., & Levinson, S. (2013b). *Usage of computer vision and machine learning to solve 3D mazes*. Urbana: University of Illinois at Urbana-Champaign.

Nath, V., & Levinson, S. (2014). Solving 3D Mazes with Machine Learning: A prelude to deep learning using the iCub Humanoid Robot. *Twenty-Eighth AAAI Conference. Quebec City: AAAI*

Russell, S., & Norvig, P. (2010). *Artificial Intelligence, A Modern Approach*. New Jersey: Prentice Hall.

Sandini, G., Metta, G., & Vernon, G. (2007). The iCub Cognitive Humanoid Robot: An Open-System Research Platform for Enactive Cognition. *In 50 years of artificial intelligence* (pp. 358–369). Berlin Heidelburg: Springer Berlin Heidelberg.

Spong, M. W., Hutchinson, S., & Vidyasagar, M. (2006). *Robot Modelling and Control*. New Jersey: John Wiley & Sons.

Tsagarakis, N., Metta, G., & Vernon, D. (2007). iCUb: The design and realization of an open humanoid platform for cognitive and neuroscience research. *Advanced Robots 21.10*, (pp. 1151–1175).

Wells, H. (2005). *The War of the Worlds*. New York: NYRB Classics.

Chapter 2
Overview of Probability and Statistics

Abstract This chapter talks about the elementary concepts of probability and statistics that are needed to better comprehend this book. This appendix covers topics like basic probability, conditional probability, Bayes' Theorem and various distributions like normal distribution (also called Gaussian distribution), Bernoulli distribution, Poisson distribution and binomial distribution.

2.1 Probability

2.1.1 Introduction

The world that we observe is a very complex one, with an infinite number of events taking place all the time, some of which are interdependent/related and some of which are independent of certain events. These events can be divided into two categories—(1) Deterministic and (2) Probabilistic. Deterministic events are those events that we are sure will happen, given the right conditions. It is the notion of cause-and-effect, in that an event A will lead to event B, when the right conditions are applied to event A. Strictly speaking, deterministic events are usually considered more of a philosophical concept than a practical one since it is impossible to predict an event with complete accuracy and confidence. There are too many variables at play in the interaction of even two systems, let alone several hundreds or thousands of them, and it would be impossible to predict the relationship between every single one of them.

However, it is important to note that the choice of granularity would depend on the event and the level of detail that the system being analyzed warrants. For example, it would be quite pointless to include calculations of atomic vibrations while flipping a biased coin, one that has heads on both sides. In this scenario, the event that the coin will result in heads can be considered a deterministic event, since we are absolutely sure that the coin will result in a heads.

The other event category are the probabilistic events. These events describe real-life scenarios more accurately because they mention the probability that an event will occur. The probability of likely events will be higher than those of unlikely events, and this variation is the measure of probability. The measure of probability is bounded by the (2.1).

$$0 \leq P(X) \leq 1 \qquad\qquad (2.1)$$

The "X" in (2.1) refers to any event X. P(X) is the notation to indicate the probability of an event "X". Equation (2.1) indicates that the minimum value of probability of any event is 0, while the maximum probability of an event is 1. This means that if an event is deemed impossible, its probability is 0, while the probability of an event that has no way of failing will be a 1.

So, what is probability? Generally speaking, probability can be thought of as the likelihood of a particular event happening. Most of us have a model of probability affecting our daily lives. For instance, we tend to look at the probability that it would rain today before deciding on taking an umbrella or not. We also use probability in a lot of trading places like the stock market. Also, the period of warranty that manufacturers indicate for a new product is an indication of the probability that the device would function for a particular duration. The probability of the device failing within the warranty period is low, and that is why the manufacturer decided to cover only up to a certain period and not for an indefinite period.

Now that we have an understanding of what is probability, let us discuss how to mathematically determine the probability of a particular event. To do this, consider one of the most widely used objects to teach probability—the board games' die. When we roll a die, there are only six numbers that can be obtained, namely 1, 2, 3, 4, 5 and 6. Representing them as a set would result in the set {1, 2, 3, 4, 5, 6}. Such a set that contains all the possible results of a particular event is called a **power set**. Thus, the set {1, 2, 3, 4, 5, 6} is the power set of the event of rolling a fair die. As an example, to determine the probability of rolling a 4 on a die can be determined as follows:

$$P(A) = \frac{\{4\}}{\{1, 2, 3, 4, 5, 6\}} = \frac{1}{6}$$

Basically, we need to have the events in the numerator and the total number of events in the denominator. As can be seen from the above equation, the probability of the die landing a 4 is 1/6. As you might have figured out by now, the probability of any number landing when a fair die is thrown is the same, i.e. 1/6. This means that when you throw a fair die, you are equally likely to get any of the six numbers marked on it.

As another commonly cited example, let us consider an ordinary coin. This coin will have two sides—a heads and a tails. What is the probability that the coin will yield heads when it is tossed? The power set of coin toss is $\{H, T\}$, where H denotes heads and T denotes tails. In this scenario,

$$P(A) = \frac{\{H\}}{\{H,T\}} = \frac{1}{2}$$

where A is the event that the coin toss will yield a heads. By a similar analysis, we can determine that the probability of a coin toss yielding a tails would also be 1/2. In other words, both the outcomes have an equal probability. Another crucial observation that can be made from both examples is that the sum of the probabilities of all the events must equal 1. This is a rule in probability and can be observed from the coin toss experiment mentioned above. The sum of both probabilities is 1/2 + 1/2 = 1. The same can be observed from the die experiment. The mathematical notation of this rule is given by (2.2) below.

$$\sum_i P(x_i) = 1 \qquad (2.2)$$

In (2.2) above, i refers to the individual events, i.e. subsets of the power set. The summation of all the individual elements would result in the power set for the event.

On a related note, there is another concept called complementary events that are a direct result of (2.2). A complementary event is an event wherein its negative will take place. For example, if an event A is defined as landing a 4 on a die roll, it's complementary event, A', would be NOT landing a 4 on a die roll. Since the sum of all the probability events must be 1, from (2.2),

$$P\left(A'\right) = 1 - P(A) = 1 - 1/6 = 5/6$$

That is, there is a 5 in 6 chance that the number obtained would not be a 4. This is in agreement with simple observation since the resultant set is $\{1, 2, 3, 5, 6\}$.

2.1.2 Conditional Probability and Bayes' Theorem

Now that we know the basics of probability, let's take a look at the topic conditional probability. Basically, conditional probability is the probability of an event when another related event has taken place. This knowledge of another related event taking place will affect our probability of the first event, and this concept is called conditional probability, in that it is the probability given a particular condition.

Let us consider the example of the die once again. The power set for an ordinary die is $\{1, 2, 3, 4, 5, 6\}$ and the probability of getting any number from 1 to 6 on a single throw is the same 1/6. However, what if I were to tell you that the die has been tampered with and that this die now contains only even numbers on it? With this new information, wouldn't the probabilities change? It surely does! In this new scenario, the power set of the die is {2, 4, 6}. Therefore, the probability of getting a 1, 3 or 5 is 0. The probability of getting a 2, 4, or 6 is 1/3. The notation for representing conditional probability is given by P(A|B) and is read as "probability of A given B". So, if we were to formalize the example we just discussed, it would be as follows:

A: Getting a 2 on a die roll
B: The die contains only even numbers

Therefore, P(A|B) = 1/3. While this approach of counting the events that satisfy a particular condition and are members of the power set might work for events with a limited number of outcomes, this approach would quickly get out of hand when we have to deal with a large number of events. It is here that the formula for conditional probability comes in handy. The formula for computing the conditional probability is given below as (2.3).

$$P(A|B) = \frac{P(A \cap B)}{P(B)} \tag{2.3}$$

To demonstrate the usage of (2.3) for determining conditional probability, let us use an example of an octahedron. An octahedron differs from a regular die in only a very small way, a regular die has six sides, while an octahedron has eight sides. So, the numbers marked on an octahedron range from 1 to 8, as opposed to 1–6 on a regular die.

Now, let us define the two events A and B as follows:

A: Getting an even number on a roll
B: Getting a number greater than 6, non-inclusive

The power set of all the rolls from an octahedron is {1, 2, 3, 4, 5, 6, 7, 8}. The probability of A = 1/2, since there is an equal chance of the roll landing in an odd or even number (the reader can also confirm this by listing all the even numbers and the power set). The set of outcomes that satisfy event B is {7, 8}. This means that the probability of B is 2/8 = 1/4. The intersection of events A and B leads to the resultant set {8}. This set satisfies both events A and B. The probability of A ∩ B = 1/8. Thus, the application of (2.3) results in the following:

$$P(A|B) = \frac{P(A \cap B)}{P(B)} = \frac{1/8}{2/8} = \frac{1}{2}$$

In this example, it so happened that P(A|B) = P(A). But this is not always necessarily true. Similarly, in this example, P(B|A) = P(B) as well. When such a condition occurs, we say that the two events A and B are **statistically independent** of each other. This means that the probability of occurrence of one event is completely independent of the probability of occurrence of another. This should make intuitive sense because when you roll an octahedron, getting an odd/even number and a number greater than 6 should not have any relationship with each other. The above equations mathematically prove this idea. Furthermore, when two events are independent, their joint probability is the product of their individual probabilities. This is shown in (2.4) below.

$$P(A \cap B) = P(A) \times P(B) \tag{2.4}$$

Conditional probability is a widely used concept in several experiments, especially because several events are related to each other in one way or the other. This concept of conditional probability and the Bayes' Theorem (which we will discuss next) is of tremendous importance to the field of artificial intelligence and is used widely in the algorithms being described in this book.

Conditional probability gives rise to another very important theorem in the field of probability, the Bayes' Theorem. The Bayes' theorem is widely used to flip the events whose probabilities are being computed, so that they can computed much more easily, and in some cases the only way they can be computed. The formula for Bayes' theorem is given by (2.5) below.

$$P(A|B) = \frac{P(B|A) \times P(A)}{P(B)} \tag{2.5}$$

As can be seen from (2.5), in the original problem we tried to compute the probability of A given B. Bayes' theorem allows us to compute this by first computing the probability of B given A, along with the individual probabilities of A and B. The Bayes' theorem of (2.5) has another form, which is given by (2.6) below.

$$P(A|B) = \frac{P(B|A) \times P(A)}{P(B)} = \frac{P(B|A) \times P(A)}{P(B|A) \times P(A) + P(B|A') \times P(A')} \tag{2.6}$$

Equation (2.6) is obtained from (2.5) by the expansion of P(B) in the denominator. This takes place because the probability of an event needs to account for the conditional probabilities of the event occurring as well as the event not occurring (complementary events). The Bayes' theorem is one of the most important theorems being used in the field of artificial intelligence, since almost all of AI deals with probabilistic events, and not deterministic events.

2.2 Probability Distributions

In this section, we will be discussing the most commonly used probability distributions. The distributions that we will discuss are Gaussian distribution, binomial distribution, Bernoulli distribution and Poisson distribution. Of course, there are various other distributions, but they are not required for an understanding of the work presented in this book and have been ignored.

Before we proceed with the distributions, there are two concepts that need to be explained to the reader to better understand the material. The first concept is that of probability mass function (PMF), while the second is called the cumulative distribution function (CDF).

PMF is a function which maps a discrete random variable as input to its corresponding probability as an output. This function is used when the inputs are purely discrete in nature (Weisstein, "Distribution Function"). For example, the ordinary 6-sided die that we discussed about has an input that is discrete in nature, i.e. it is guaranteed to be a natural number between 1 and 6. As shown previously, the probability of each of the inputs being obtained for a fair die is equal, which is 1/6. Thus, if one were to plot the pmf of the inputs of a die, it would be six equal line segments that represent a value of 1/6 each. Similarly, for a single fair coin toss, the only two outcomes would be heads and tails. Therefore, if we were to obtain the pmf of this event, it would be two equal line segments that represent a value of 1/2 each.

CDF is a similar function as PMF, with the difference that this function gives the sum of all the possible probabilities until that event has been reached. For continuous functions, the CDF would range from negative infinity to the point where the current event of interest has been obtained/plotted on the graph (Weisstein). Both the PMF and CDF have been shown in the distributions being discussed for certain cases, as an example.

2.2.1 Gaussian Distribution

The Gaussian distribution is one of the most commonly used probability distribution function, and is also called the normal distribution. The Gaussian distribution is also referred to as the bell curve because of the shape of the PMF function of the normal distribution (the bell curve has a lot of applications while grading tests since professors tend to "curve" the grades based on overall class performance). The Gaussian distribution has a number of parameters that are needed to accurately model it. The first one is μ, which is also called the *mean* of the distribution. The mean is the sum of all the random variables in the distribution times the probability of each of the random variables. This can be represented in equation form below, as (2.7) (Weisstein, "Normal Distribution").

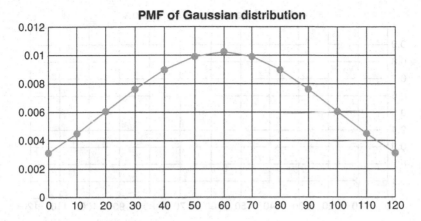

Fig. 2.1 PMF of Gaussian distribution

$$\mu = \sum_x x\, P(x) \tag{2.7}$$

The other parameter is σ, the *standard deviation* of the distribution. Standard deviation is a measure of the variation of the members of the distribution from the mean (Weisstein, "Normal Distribution") and is given by (2.8).

$$\sigma = \sqrt{\frac{1}{N}\sum_{i=1}^{N}(x_i - \mu)^2} \tag{2.8}$$

In (2.8), each value of x is a member of the distribution. σ^2 is also called the *variance* of the distribution.

Now that we have the required parameters to accurately represent the Gaussian distribution, the PMF of a Gaussian distribution is given by (2.9), while the CDF is given by (2.10) below (Weisstein).

$$PMF = \frac{1}{\sigma\sqrt{2\pi}}e^{\frac{-(x-\mu)^2}{2\sigma^2}} \tag{2.9}$$

$$CDF = \frac{1}{2}\left[1 + \operatorname{erf}\left(\frac{x-\mu}{\sqrt{2\sigma^2}}\right)\right] \tag{2.10}$$

Figures 2.1 and 2.2 show the PMF and CDF of a Gaussian distribution.

One last thing before concluding the section on Gaussian distribution, when $\mu = 0$ and $\sigma = 1$, the distribution can also be called the *standard normal distribution*.

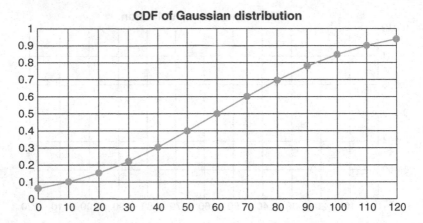

Fig. 2.2 CDF of Gaussian distribution

2.2.2 *Binomial Distribution*

The binomial distribution is another type of distribution that is very commonly encountered when the same experiment is repeated several times. The experiment is of the pass/fail or yes/no type, where the probability of success is denoted by a parameter, say "p". Since the outcome of these experiments is comprised of two possibilities, the probability of failure would be 1 − p. This is because of the complementary nature of the success and failure of the events.

The binomial distribution is the distribution used to model the repeated tossing of a coin, rolling a die, or any other such experiment, where it would be extremely hard to model the event using other models. The PMF of a binomial distribution is given by (2.11) below (Weisstein, "Binomial Distribution").

$$PMF = {}^{n}_{s}C\,p^{s}(1-p)^{n-s} \tag{2.11}$$

In (2.11), s is the number of successes that the experiment yielded, or we would like to yield. Since the total number of iterations of the experiment is n, the number of failures of the experiment has to be (n − s). This is the term that is the super-script of the term (1 − p), in (2.11), since (1 − p) denotes the probability of failure.

Lastly, if X is a random variable, then the expected value of X is given by (2.12) and its variance is given by (2.13) below (Weisstein).

$$E[X] = np \tag{2.12}$$

$$Var(X) = np(1-p) \tag{2.13}$$

As an example, assume a fair coin is tossed 100 times. The definition of a fair coin, as discussed previously, is a coin that has an equal probability of yielding a

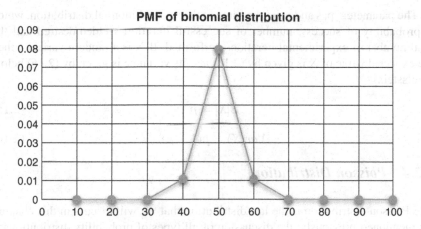

Fig. 2.3 PMF of binomial distribution of a fair coin for 100 times

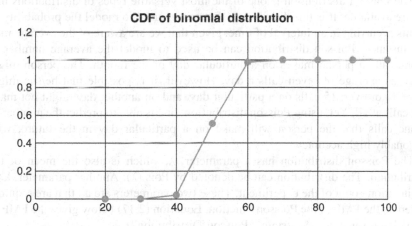

Fig. 2.4 CDF of binomial distribution of a fair coin for 100 times

heads or a tails when tossed, with the probability being 1/2. Figures 2.3 and 2.4 above show the PMF and CDF of this binomial distribution experiment.

2.2.3 Bernoulli Distribution

The Bernoulli distribution is a special case of the binomial distribution. In the binomial distribution, when n = 1, it is the Bernoulli distribution. The pmf of the Bernoulli distribution is given by (2.14) below (Weisstein, "Bernoulli Distribution").

$$PMF = p^s (1-p)^{n-s} \tag{2.14}$$

The parameters p, s and n are the same as that of the binomial distribution, which is probability of success, number of successful iteration yielded/desired and the total number of experimental iterations performed. If X is a random variable, then the expected value of X is given by (2.15) and its variance is given by (2.16) below (Weisstein).

$$E[X] = p \tag{2.15}$$

$$Var(X) = p(1 - p) \tag{2.16}$$

2.2.4 Poisson Distribution

The Poisson distribution is the last distribution that we will discuss in this chapter. As mentioned previously, the discussion of all types of probability distributions is beyond the scope of this book.

The Poisson distribution is one of the most versatile types of distributions that we are available. It is this distribution that can be used to model the probability of events occurring in an interval of time, given that we are aware of the average rate. For instance, Poisson distribution can be used to model the average number of phone calls a person makes on a particular day of the month. The person might make an average of seven calls a day. However, it is possible that he/she might make 10 or even 15 calls on a particular day, and on another day might not make any calls at all. Yet, using Poisson distribution, one is able to predict the number of phone calls that the person will make on a particular day in the future, with reasonably high accuracy.

The Poisson distribution has a parameter, λ, which is also the mean of the distribution. The distribution can be denoted by Pois (λ). Another parameter, k, is the iteration count of the experiment. These two parameters are all that are required to denote the PMF of the Poisson function. Equation (2.17) below gives the PMF of the Poisson function (Weisstein, "Poisson Distribution").

$$PMF = \frac{e^{-\lambda}\lambda^k}{k!} \tag{2.17}$$

If X is a random variable, then the expected value of X is given by (2.18) and its variance is given by (2.19) below (Weisstein, "Poisson Distribution").

$$E[X] = \lambda \tag{2.18}$$

$$Var(X) = \lambda \tag{2.19}$$

Figures 2.5 and 2.6 below show the PMF and CDF of a Poisson distribution with $\lambda = 7.5$.

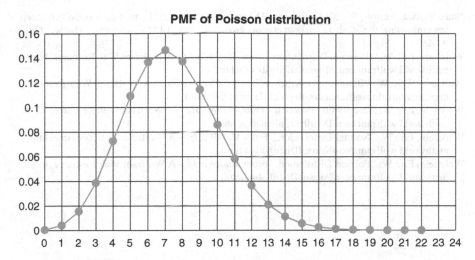

Fig. 2.5 PMF of Poisson distribution

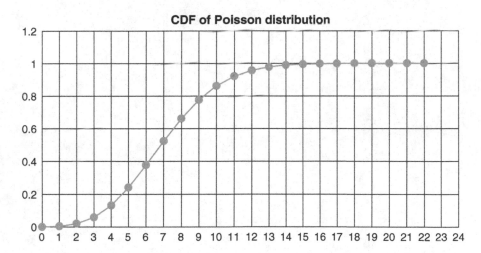

Fig. 2.6 CDF of Poisson distribution

References

Barber, D. (2012). *Bayesian Reasoning and Machine Learning*. Cambridge: University Press.
Forsyth, D., & Ponce. (2011). *Computer Vision: A Modern Approach*. Prentice Hall.
Nath, V., & Levinson, S. (2013a). Learning to Fire at Targets by an iCub Humanoid Robot. *AAAI Spring Symposium*. Palo Alto: AAAI.
Nath, V., & Levinson, S. (2013b). *Usage of computer vision and machine learning to solve 3D mazes*. Urbana: University of Illinois at Urbana-Champaign.

Nath, V., & Levinson, S. (2014). Solving 3D Mazes with Machine Learning: A prelude to deep learning using the iCub Humanoid Robot. *Twenty-Eighth AAAI Conference. Quebec City: AAAI*

Weisstein, Eric W. "Binomial Distribution." From *MathWorld* – A Wolfram Web Resource. http://mathworld.wolfram.com/BinomialDistribution.html

Weisstein, Eric W. "Bernoulli Distribution." From *MathWorld* – A Wolfram Web Resource. http://mathworld.wolfram.com/BernoulliDistribution.html

Weisstein, Eric W. "Distribution Function." From *MathWorld* – A Wolfram Web Resource. http://mathworld.wolfram.com/DistributionFunction.html

Weisstein, Eric W. "Normal Distribution." From *MathWorld* – A Wolfram Web Resource. http://mathworld.wolfram.com/NormalDistribution.html

Weisstein, Eric W. "Poisson Distribution." From *MathWorld* – A Wolfram Web Resource. http://mathworld.wolfram.com/PoissonDistribution.html

Chapter 3
Primer on Matrices and Determinants

Abstract In this chapter, we will be covering the basic concepts of matrices, determinants and, eigenvalues and eigenvectors in this chapter. If the reader is familiar with these concepts, then the reader can skip ahead to the next chapter without any loss of continuity.

3.1 Matrices

Matrices can be thought of as a collection of numbers, or a group of numbers, or even expressions, arranged in rows and columns. Matrices are usually rectangular in shape, although at times they can also be square in shape. Matrices are a very common way of representing a group of related numbers together, as a measurement, or to express relationships between measurements.

Each individual number or expression in a matrix is called an *element*. We just mentioned that a matrix contains rows and columns. If a matrix contains m rows and n columns, we say that the matrix has an *order of m by n*. The order of a matrix is of crucial importance in matrix operations since the size and shape of a matrix is described by the order. Furthermore, it is very important to remember that a matrix of order m by n is completely different from a matrix of order n by m. Lastly, matrices are bound by squares, but some people prefer parentheses. It doesn't matter which style the reader chooses, it is more a matter of aesthetics and not a matter of importance.

The matrix $\begin{bmatrix} 1 & 2 & 3 \\ 4 & 5 & 6 \\ 7 & 8 & 9 \end{bmatrix}$ has three rows and three columns, and therefore has an

order of 3 by 3. On the other hand, the matrix $\begin{bmatrix} 1 & 2 \\ 3 & 4 \end{bmatrix}$ has two rows and two

V. Nath and S.E. Levinson, *Autonomous Robotics and Deep Learning*, SpringerBriefs in Computer Science, DOI 10.1007/978-3-319-05603-6_3, © The Author(s) 2014

columns, and therefore has an order of 2 by 2. Each element in the matrix can be uniquely identified and referenced to.

The following chart shows the arrangement of elements in a 3 by 3 matrix—
$\begin{bmatrix} a_{11} & a_{12} & a_{13} \\ a_{21} & a_{22} & a_{23} \\ a_{31} & a_{32} & a_{33} \end{bmatrix}$. As can be seen, the subscript denotes the position of the element that is being referenced, with the first number referring to the row position while the second number refers to the column position. For instance, a_{32} refers to the third row and second column, while a_{13} refers to the first row and the third column. Thus, in the aforementioned example, for the 3 by 3 matrix, $a_{11} = 1$, $a_{13} = 3$, $a_{22} = 5$, $a_{31} = 7$ and $a_{33} = 9$. In this way, every single element of any matrix can be determined and referenced without any confusion.

There are certain types of special matrices, special with regards to their size. Some matrices can have any number of rows, but only one column. They have an order of n by 1, and are called *column vectors* since they consist of only a single column. An example of a column vector is the matrix $\begin{bmatrix} 10 \\ 20 \\ 30 \end{bmatrix}$. Some matrices can have any number of columns, but only one row. These matrices have an order of 1 by n, and are called *row vectors* since they consist of just one row. An example of a row matrix is $\begin{bmatrix} 25 & 30 & 32 \end{bmatrix}$. Just to reiterate, the number of columns in a column vector and the number of rows in a row vector is unbounded, i.e. can be as large as required. There are certain matrices that have the same number of rows and columns. Such matrices have an order of n by n, and are also called square matrices, since they resemble the shape of a square with equal length and breadth. The matrix that was discussed previously, $\begin{bmatrix} 1 & 2 & 3 \\ 4 & 5 & 6 \\ 7 & 8 & 9 \end{bmatrix}$, is an example of a square matrix. Of course, even here, the number of rows and columns don't have a maximum number. The matrix, $\begin{bmatrix} 15 & 16 & -2 & 45 \\ 0 & 99 & 56 & 7 \\ 3 & 21 & 78 & -13 \\ -1 & 17 & 81 & 22 \end{bmatrix}$, with an order of 4 by 4, also fits the definition and is a square matrix.

In order to perform certain matrix operations, the order of the matrices involved are important, like addition and multiplication. In order to perform matrix addition between matrices, it is a requirement that both matrices must have the same order. So, in order for a matrix to be added to another matrix of order 3 by 2, the first matrix must also have an order of 3 by 2. If the order of the two matrices are the same, then it is simply a matter of addition of elements having the same position in the two matrices. The following examples should make matrix addition clear to the reader.

1. $\begin{bmatrix} 1 & 2 & 3 \\ 4 & 5 & 6 \\ 7 & 8 & 9 \end{bmatrix} + \begin{bmatrix} 10 & 3 & 0 \\ -2 & 9 & 1 \\ 19 & 16 & 3 \end{bmatrix} = \begin{bmatrix} 11 & 5 & 3 \\ 2 & 14 & 7 \\ 26 & 24 & 12 \end{bmatrix}$

2. $\begin{bmatrix} 1 & 2 \\ 3 & 4 \end{bmatrix} + \begin{bmatrix} 9 & 3 \\ 4 & -1 \end{bmatrix} = \begin{bmatrix} 10 & 5 \\ 7 & 3 \end{bmatrix}$

3. $\begin{bmatrix} 15 & 16 & -2 & 45 \\ 0 & 99 & 56 & 7 \\ 3 & 21 & 78 & -13 \\ -1 & 17 & 81 & 22 \end{bmatrix} + \begin{bmatrix} 1 & 2 & 3 \\ 4 & 5 & 6 \\ 7 & 8 & 9 \end{bmatrix}$

= NOT POSSIBLE (ORDER MISMATCH)

Hopefully, the reader is now clear about matrix addition. The next operation is that of scalar multiplication of a matrix. The scalar multiplication of a matrix is the operation wherein a matrix is multiplied with a number. The resultant matrix is obtained when each element of the matrix is multiplied by the scalar. The following examples should hopefully throw some light on this topic for the reader.

1. $3 \times \begin{bmatrix} 1 & 2 & 3 \\ 4 & 5 & 6 \\ 7 & 8 & 9 \end{bmatrix} = \begin{bmatrix} 3 \times 1 & 3 \times 2 & 3 \times 3 \\ 3 \times 4 & 3 \times 5 & 3 \times 6 \\ 3 \times 7 & 3 \times 8 & 3 \times 9 \end{bmatrix} = \begin{bmatrix} 3 & 6 & 9 \\ 12 & 15 & 18 \\ 21 & 24 & 27 \end{bmatrix}$

2. $-2 \times \begin{bmatrix} 9 & 3 \\ 4 & -1 \end{bmatrix} = \begin{bmatrix} -2 \times 9 & -2 \times 3 \\ -2 \times 4 & -2 \times -1 \end{bmatrix} = \begin{bmatrix} -18 & -6 \\ -8 & 2 \end{bmatrix}$.

Another major operation that needs to be discussed is the determination of the *transpose* of a matrix. The transpose of a matrix A is denoted by A^T. The transpose of a m by n matrix would result in a matrix with order n by m and the resultant matrix is obtained by turning all the rows of matrix A into the columns of the transpose matrix and turning all the columns of matrix A into the rows of the transpose matrix. As the keen reader would have observed by now, the transpose of a square matrix would result in a matrix with the same order as the original matrix.

1. $\begin{bmatrix} 1 & 2 & 3 \\ 4 & 5 & 6 \\ 7 & 8 & 9 \end{bmatrix}^T = \begin{bmatrix} 1 & 4 & 7 \\ 2 & 5 & 8 \\ 3 & 6 & 9 \end{bmatrix}$

2. $\begin{bmatrix} 9 & 3 \\ 4 & -1 \end{bmatrix}^T = \begin{bmatrix} 9 & 4 \\ 3 & -1 \end{bmatrix}$

3. $\begin{bmatrix} 15 & 16 & -2 & 45 \\ 0 & 99 & 56 & 7 \\ 3 & 21 & 78 & -13 \\ -1 & 17 & 81 & 22 \end{bmatrix}^T = \begin{bmatrix} 15 & 0 & 3 & -1 \\ 16 & 99 & 21 & 17 \\ -2 & 56 & 78 & 81 \\ 45 & 7 & -13 & 22 \end{bmatrix}$

Another major matrix operation that we would discuss in this chapter is that of matrix multiplication. Matrix multiplication has a unique requirement that is different from the requirements of any of the previous requirements. The requirement is that the number of columns of the first matrix must be equal to the number of rows of the second matrix. In other words, if the order of the first matrix is m by n, then the order of the second matrix would be n by x, where x could or could not be equal to x. When these matrices are multiplied together, the resultant matrix would lead to a matrix of order m by x. In order to make things simple, the reader can imagine the two n's cancelling each other out when the two orders are being multiplied.

Once the requirements for the matrix multiplication have been satisfied, we can proceed with the actual multiplication. Basically, the first element of the resultant matrix is obtained by the piecewise multiplication of the first row of the first matrix with the left-most column of the second matrix. The second element on the first row is obtained by the multiplication of the first row of the first matrix with the second left-most column of the second matrix. This same scaling is also needed for the rows as well. In this manner, each element of the resultant matrix needs to be computed. The following examples would help the reader understand the concept of matrix multiplication better.

1. $\begin{bmatrix} 1 & 2 & 3 \\ 4 & 5 & 6 \\ 7 & 8 & 9 \end{bmatrix} \times \begin{bmatrix} 1 & 4 & 7 \\ 2 & 5 & 8 \\ 3 & 6 & 9 \end{bmatrix}$

$= \begin{bmatrix} 1 \times 1 + 2 \times 2 + 3 \times 3 & 1 \times 4 + 2 \times 5 + 3 \times 6 & 1 \times 7 + 2 \times 8 + 3 \times 9 \\ 4 \times 1 + 5 \times 2 + 6 \times 3 & 4 \times 4 + 5 \times 5 + 6 \times 6 & 4 \times 7 + 5 \times 8 + 6 \times 9 \\ 7 \times 1 + 8 \times 2 + 9 \times 3 & 7 \times 4 + 8 \times 5 + 9 \times 6 & 7 \times 7 + 8 \times 8 + 9 \times 9 \end{bmatrix}$

$= \begin{bmatrix} 1 + 4 + 9 & 4 + 10 + 18 & 7 + 16 + 27 \\ 4 + 10 + 18 & 16 + 25 + 36 & 28 + 40 + 54 \\ 7 + 16 + 27 & 28 + 40 + 54 & 49 + 64 + 81 \end{bmatrix}$

$= \begin{bmatrix} 14 & 32 & 50 \\ 32 & 77 & 122 \\ 50 & 122 & 194 \end{bmatrix}$

2. $\begin{bmatrix} 9 & 3 \\ 4 & -1 \end{bmatrix} \times \begin{bmatrix} 1 & 2 \\ 3 & 4 \end{bmatrix} = \begin{bmatrix} 9 \times 1 + 3 \times 3 & 9 \times 2 + 3 \times 4 \\ 4 \times 1 + -1 \times 3 & 4 \times 2 + -1 \times 4 \end{bmatrix}$

$= \begin{bmatrix} 9+9 & 18+12 \\ 4-3 & 8-4 \end{bmatrix} = \begin{bmatrix} 18 & 30 \\ 1 & 4 \end{bmatrix}$

3. $\begin{bmatrix} 1 & 4 & 7 \\ 2 & 5 & 8 \\ 3 & 6 & 9 \end{bmatrix} \times \begin{bmatrix} 10 \\ 20 \\ 30 \end{bmatrix} = \begin{bmatrix} 1 \times 10 + 4 \times 20 + 7 \times 30 \\ 2 \times 10 + 5 \times 20 + 8 \times 30 \\ 3 \times 10 + 6 \times 20 + 9 \times 30 \end{bmatrix}$

$= \begin{bmatrix} 10+80+210 \\ 20+100+240 \\ 30+120+270 \end{bmatrix} = \begin{bmatrix} 300 \\ 360 \\ 420 \end{bmatrix}$

4. $\begin{bmatrix} 15 & 16 & -2 & 45 \\ 0 & 99 & 56 & 7 \\ 3 & 21 & 78 & -13 \\ -1 & 17 & 81 & 22 \end{bmatrix} \times \begin{bmatrix} 1 & 4 & 7 \\ 2 & 5 & 8 \\ 3 & 6 & 9 \end{bmatrix}$

= NOT POSSIBLE (ORDER MISMATCH)

With these examples, we conclude the section on matrix multiplication. The last major matrix operation that we would discuss in this chapter is that of finding the inverse of a matrix.

For a square matrix **A**, the following (3.1) needs to be followed, to determine its inverse (Weisstein).

$$AA^{-1} = A^{-1}A = I \tag{3.1}$$

The inverse of a matrix **A** is denoted by A^{-1}. The **I** seen in (3.1) is the identity matrix, a square matrix whose elements are all 1 on the main diagonal and 0 everywhere else. For example, the 3 × 3 identity matrix is given below.

$$\begin{bmatrix} 1 & 0 & 0 \\ 0 & 1 & 0 \\ 0 & 0 & 1 \end{bmatrix}$$

For a 2 × 2 matrix $\begin{bmatrix} a & b \\ c & d \end{bmatrix}$, in order to determine its inverse, we use (3.1) and end up with (3.2) (Weisstein).

$$\begin{bmatrix} a & b \\ c & d \end{bmatrix}^{-1} = \frac{1}{ad - bc} \begin{bmatrix} d & -b \\ -c & a \end{bmatrix} \tag{3.2}$$

As an example, we will compute the inverse of the matrix $\begin{bmatrix} 1 & 2 \\ 3 & 4 \end{bmatrix}$.

$$\begin{bmatrix} 1 & 2 \\ 3 & 4 \end{bmatrix}^{-1} = \frac{1}{1 \times 4 - 2 \times 3} \begin{bmatrix} 4 & -2 \\ -3 & 1 \end{bmatrix} = \frac{1}{4-6} \begin{bmatrix} 4 & -2 \\ -3 & 1 \end{bmatrix}$$

$$= \frac{1}{-2} \begin{bmatrix} 4 & -2 \\ -3 & 1 \end{bmatrix} = \begin{bmatrix} -2 & 1 \\ 3/2 & -1/2 \end{bmatrix}$$

For 3 × 3 matrices and other matrices of greater orders, the process of computing the inverse of a matrix would still require the satisfaction of (3.1). However, it
would be quite cumbersome to determine the inverse this way. Fortunately, there
are other ways to determine the inverse using methods like the Gauss-Jordan
method, or using minors, cofactors, etc. (Weisstein). The discussion of these topics
is beyond the scope of this book and is not covered here.

3.2 Determinants

For a given *square matrix A*, the determinant is the volume of the transformation of
the matrix A. This means that we take a hypercube of unit volume and map each
vertex under the transformation, and the volume of the resultant object is defined as
a determinant (Barber 2012). Thus, the determinant of $\begin{bmatrix} 1 & 4 & 7 \\ 2 & 5 & 8 \\ 3 & 6 & 9 \end{bmatrix}$ can be
computed because it is a square matrix, while the determinant of $\begin{bmatrix} 10 \\ 20 \\ 30 \end{bmatrix}$ cannot
be computed because it is not a square matrix.

Let us assume a generic 3 × 3 matrix $\begin{bmatrix} a & b & c \\ d & e & f \\ g & h & i \end{bmatrix}$ and we shall determine its
determinant. The determinant of this square matrix is written as $\begin{vmatrix} a & b & c \\ d & e & f \\ g & h & i \end{vmatrix}$,
i.e. with vertical bars to denote that we are trying to determine the determinant of
the matrix. The determinant of a matrix **A** is denoted by det(**A**) or also |**A**|. The
determinant of this matrix is given by the following equation.

$$a(e \times i - f \times h) - b(d \times i - f \times g) + c(d \times h - e \times g)$$

One thing to point out here is that the signs keep altering for alternating elements. The following examples would help the reader better understand the concept of determining the determinant of a matrix.

1.

$$\begin{vmatrix} 1 & 4 & 7 \\ 2 & 5 & 8 \\ 3 & 6 & 9 \end{vmatrix}$$

$$= 1(5 \times 9 - 8 \times 6) - 4(2 \times 9 - 8 \times 3) + 7(2 \times 6 - 5 \times 3)$$
$$= 1(45 - 48) - 4(18 - 24) + 7(12 - 15) = 1 \times (-3) + -4 \times (-6) + 7 \times (-3)$$
$$= -3 + 24 - 21 = 0$$

2.

$$\begin{bmatrix} 1 & 0 & 0 \\ 0 & 1 & 0 \\ 0 & 0 & 1 \end{bmatrix}$$

$$= 1(1 \times 1 - 0 \times 0) - 0(0 \times 1 - 0 \times 0) + 0(0 \times 0 - 1 \times 0)$$
$$= 1 - 0 + 0$$
$$= 1$$

Of interest to note is that $\det(\mathbf{A}^T) = \det(\mathbf{A})$. Also, if two square matrices $\mathbf{A}$ and $\mathbf{B}$ are of equal dimensions, then $\det(\mathbf{AB}) = \det(\mathbf{A}) \times \det(\mathbf{B})$. This section concludes a brief overview of determinants. The last section of this chapter deals with eigenvalues and eigenvectors.

3.3 Eigenvalues and Eigenvectors

The eigenvectors of a given matrix $\mathbf{A}$ correspond to a coordinate system in which the geometric transformation represented by $\mathbf{A}$ is best understood. Geometrically speaking, the eigenvectors are special directions such that the effect of the transformation $\mathbf{A}$ along a direction $\mathbf{e}$ would be to scale $\mathbf{e}$ (Barber 2012). For a square matrix $\mathbf{a}$ of order n by n, $\mathbf{e}$ is an eigenvector of $\mathbf{a}$ with eigenvalue λ if (3.3) is satisfied.

$$ae = \lambda e \tag{3.3}$$

Equation (3.3) can be re-written as $(\mathbf{a} - \lambda \times \mathbf{I})\mathbf{e} = \mathbf{0}$. This equation would have a solution if $\mathbf{e} = \mathbf{0}$, i.e. $(\mathbf{a} - \lambda \times \mathbf{I})$ is invertible. In this form, the solution is trivial. There is another possibility wherein $(\mathbf{a} - \lambda \times \mathbf{I})$ is non-invertible i.e. has a non-zero determinant. Therefore, λ becomes an eigenvalue of $\mathbf{a}$ if:

$$|\mathbf{a} - \lambda \times \mathbf{I}| = 0 \tag{3.4}$$

Equation (3.4) is also known as the characteristic equation. A deeper discussion of eigenvalues and eigenvectors is not required for the understanding of the material presented in this book and is being omitted here for the sake of brevity.

References

Barber, D. (2012). *Bayesian Reasoning and Machine Learning*. Cambridge: University Press.

Nath, V., & Levinson, S. (2013a). Learning to Fire at Targets by an iCub Humanoid Robot. *AAAI Spring Symposium*. Palo Alto: AAAI.

Nath, V., & Levinson, S. (2013b). *Usage of computer vision and machine learning to solve 3D mazes*. Urbana: University of Illinois at Urbana-Champaign.

Nath, V., & Levinson, S. (2014). Solving 3D Mazes with Machine Learning: A prelude to deep learning using the iCub Humanoid Robot. *Twenty-Eighth AAAI Conference. Quebec City: AAAI*

Russell, S., & Norvig, P. (2010). *Artificial Intelligence, A Modern Approach*. New Jersey: Prentice Hall.

Weisstein, Eric W. "Matrix Inverse." From *MathWorld* – A Wolfram Web Resource. http://mathworld.wolfram.com/MatrixInverse.html

Weisstein, Eric W. "Matrix." From *MathWorld* – A Wolfram Web Resource. http://mathworld.wolfram.com/Matrix.html

Chapter 4
Robot Kinematics

Abstract The robotic platform is the physical hardware on which the experiments have been conducted. All algorithms, by definition, should be replicable on any physical machine, irrespective of the individual hardware components. However, all other things being constant, there is no denying that algorithms perform better on more capable hardware. In this chapter, we provide an introduction to the physical characteristics of the iCub robot platform that was used to perform the experiments and benchmark it using parameters that are relevant to the domain of robotics.

4.1 iCub Physical Description

The iCub robot is a humanoid robot that is the result of RobotCub, a collaborative project funded by the European Commission under the sixth framework programme (FP6) by Unit E5: Cognitive Systems, Interaction and Robotics. While creating an open hardware and software platform in humanoid robotics is one of the goals of the RobotCub, the primary goal of the RobotCub project is to advance the current understanding of natural and artificial cognitive systems (Metta et al. 2008).

Standing at 1.04 m (3.41 ft) tall, the iCub is the size of a three and half year old child. The iCub is able to perform a variety of physical feats like crawling on all fours, grasp small objects like balls, etc. (Nath and Levinson 2013a, b). RobotCub's stance on cognition is that manipulation of objects by an agent plays a fundamental role in the development of its cognitive ability (Metta et al. 2008). However, most of such basic skills, many of which we take for granted, are not present at birth, but rather developed through ontogenesis (Metta et al. 2008). Ideally speaking, the iCub robot would push the boundaries of human understanding of cognitive development, and the primary method of doing so would be to get the iCub to interact with objects around it.

V. Nath and S.E. Levinson, *Autonomous Robotics and Deep Learning*, SpringerBriefs in Computer Science, DOI 10.1007/978-3-319-05603-6_4, © The Author(s) 2014

The iCub has a total of 53 degrees of freedom (DOF), of which 30 DOF are present in the torso region. Each hand has 9 DOF with three independent fingers, and the fourth and fifth fingers have 1 DOF each since they are to be used only for providing additional stability and support. Each leg has 6 DOF and are strong enough to allow bipedal locomotion. The iCub also has a wide array of force and torque sensors, digital cameras, gyroscopes and accelerometers present inside. The low-level control loop is handled by a set of DSP-based control cards, and they all have the ability to perform full-duplex communication with each other using the CAN protocol. All the sensory and motor information is processed using an embedded Pentium-based PC104 controller. For the resource intensive operations, the computation is performed on an external cluster of machines that is connected to the iCub using a gigabit (1 Gb = 10^9 bits, i.e. a billion bits) Ethernet connection (Metta et al. 2008).

4.2   DH Parameters of the iCub

A frame of reference is required to describe any physical system. One of the most commonly used convention for selecting frames of reference in robots is the Denavit-Hartenberg convention, also called the DH convention. The DH convention involves four parameters—α, θ, a and d. The names of the parameters are given below:

1. α—Link twist
2. θ—Joint angle
3. a—Link length
4. d—Link Offset

The four parameters are associated with a particular link and a particular joint. The parameter "d" is for prismatic joints, while the parameter "θ" is for revolute joints (Spong et al. 2006). The iCub documentation provides the DH parameters for the right hand of the iCub robot. They have been reproduced in Table 4.1 below.

Table 4.1 DH parameters of the right arm of the iCub (Nath and Levinson 2013a, b)

Link	a	d	α	θ
1	32	0	$\pi/2$	0
2	0	−5.5	$\pi/2$	−$\pi/2$
3	−23.467	−143.3	$\pi/2$	−$\pi/2$
4	0	−107.74	$\pi/2$	−$\pi/2$
5	0	0	−$\pi/2$	−$\pi/2$
6	−15	−152.28	−$\pi/2$	−$\pi/2$
7	15	0	$\pi/2$	$\pi/2$
8	0	−137.3	$\pi/2$	−$\pi/2$
9	0	0	$\pi/2$	$\pi/2$
10	62.5	16	0	π

These parameters are all components of every homogenous transformation, denoted by A. The homogenous transformation is represented as the product of four transformations, and is explained below (Spong et al. 2006).

$$A_i = Rot_{z,\theta_i} Trans_{z,d_i} Trans_{x,a_i} Rot_{x,\alpha_i}$$

$$= \begin{bmatrix} c\theta_i & -s\theta_i & 0 & 0 \\ s\theta_i & c\theta_i & 0 & 0 \\ 0 & 0 & 1 & 0 \\ 0 & 0 & 0 & 1 \end{bmatrix} \begin{bmatrix} 1 & 0 & 0 & 0 \\ 0 & 1 & 0 & 0 \\ 0 & 0 & 1 & d_i \\ 0 & 0 & 0 & 1 \end{bmatrix} \begin{bmatrix} 1 & 0 & 0 & a_i \\ 0 & 1 & 0 & 0 \\ 0 & 0 & 1 & 0 \\ 0 & 0 & 0 & 1 \end{bmatrix} \begin{bmatrix} 1 & 0 & 0 & 0 \\ 0 & c\alpha_i & -s\alpha_i & 0 \\ 0 & s\alpha_i & c\alpha_i & 0 \\ 0 & 0 & 0 & 1 \end{bmatrix}$$

$$= \begin{bmatrix} c\theta_i & -s\theta_i c\alpha_i & s\theta_i s\alpha_i & c\theta_i \\ s\theta_i & c\theta_i c\alpha_i & -c\theta_i s\alpha_i & a_i s\theta_i \\ 0 & s\alpha_i & c\alpha_i & d_i \\ 0 & 0 & 0 & 1 \end{bmatrix}$$

(4.1)

The homogenous transformation matrix that expresses the position and orientation of a set of coordinate frames with that of another set of coordinate frames is called the transformation matrix (Spong et al. 2006). If the transformation matrix expresses the set of coordinate frames j with the set i, the transformation matrix can be denoted as T_j^i, wherein

$$\begin{aligned} T_j^i &= A_{i+1} A_{i+2} \ldots, \text{if } i < j \\ &= I, \qquad\qquad \text{if } i = j \\ &= \left(T_j^i\right)^{-1}, \qquad \text{if } j > i \end{aligned}$$

(4.2)

The origin of the frame of the frame of reference for the iCub robot is at the intersection point of the torso and the legs of the robot (Sandini et al. 2007). Furthermore, the iCub needs to hold out its right hand so that it can begin to solve the maze. Based on the schematics and information that were provided in the iCub documentation, we determined that the transformation matrices for ten links would be needed, i.e. the computation of T_{10}^0 is needed. The computation was done in accordance with (4.1) and (4.2) and the results are given below.

$$T_1^0 = \begin{vmatrix} 0 & 0 & -1 & 32 \\ 0 & -1 & 0 & 5.5 \\ -1 & 0 & 0 & 0 \\ 0 & 0 & 0 & 1 \end{vmatrix}$$

$$T_2^0 = \begin{vmatrix} 0 & -1 & 0 & 175.3 \\ 1 & 0 & 0 & -17.967 \\ 0 & 0 & 1 & 0 \\ 0 & 0 & 0 & 1 \end{vmatrix}$$

$$T_3^0 = \begin{vmatrix} 1 & 0 & 0 & 175.3 \\ 0 & 0 & -1 & -17.967 \\ 0 & 1 & 0 & -107.74 \\ 0 & 0 & 0 & 1 \end{vmatrix}$$

$$T_4^0 = \begin{vmatrix} 0 & 0 & 1 & 175.3 \\ 0 & 1 & 0 & -17.967 \\ -1 & 0 & 0 & -107.74 \\ 0 & 0 & 0 & 1 \end{vmatrix}$$

$$T_5^0 = \begin{vmatrix} 0 & -1 & 0 & 175.3 \\ -1 & 0 & 0 & -17.967 \\ 0 & 0 & -1 & -107.74 \\ 0 & 0 & 0 & 1 \end{vmatrix}$$

$$T_6^0 = \begin{vmatrix} 1 & 0 & 0 & 160.3 \\ 0 & 0 & -1 & -17.967 \\ 0 & 1 & 0 & 44.54 \\ 0 & 0 & 0 & 1 \end{vmatrix}$$

$$T_7^0 = \begin{vmatrix} 0 & 0 & 1 & 160.3 \\ 0 & -1 & 0 & -17.967 \\ 1 & 0 & 0 & 59.54 \\ 0 & 0 & 0 & 1 \end{vmatrix}$$

$$T_8^0 = \begin{vmatrix} 0 & 1 & 0 & 23 \\ 1 & 0 & 0 & -17.967 \\ 0 & 0 & -1 & 59.54 \\ 0 & 0 & 0 & 1 \end{vmatrix}$$

$$T_9^0 = \begin{vmatrix} 1 & 0 & 0 & 23 \\ 0 & 0 & 1 & -17.967 \\ 0 & -1 & 0 & 59.54 \\ 0 & 0 & 0 & 1 \end{vmatrix}$$

$$T_{10}^0 = \begin{vmatrix} -1 & 0 & 0 & -39.5 \\ 0 & 0 & 1 & -1.967 \\ 0 & 1 & 0 & 59.54 \\ 0 & 0 & 0 & 1 \end{vmatrix}$$

By using these transformation matrices, along with the DH parameters of the right arm, we have all the information that is needed to get the right arm up to slightly less than the shoulder level, getting it to the ideal level for solving the maze.

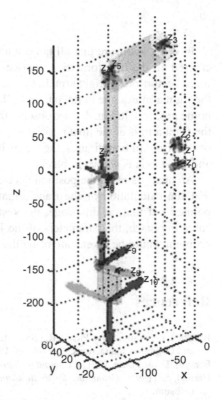

Fig. 4.1 Position vectors of the right arm of the iCub at home position (Nath and Levinson 2013a, b)

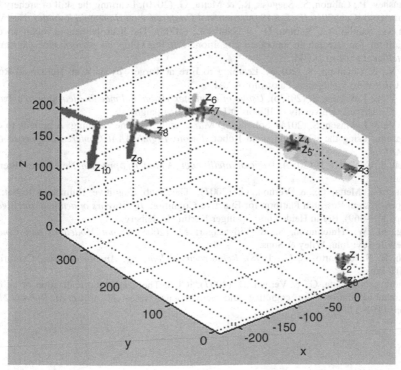

Fig. 4.2 Position vectors of the right arm of the iCub at the final position (Nath and Levinson 2013a, b)

In order to ensure that all the calculations have been performed accurately, we entered all the transformation matrices into a MATLAB simulator to observe the force vectors on the right arm. In Fig. 4.1, we observe the force vectors at the instant the right arm is at the initial phase, i.e. hanging by the torso from the shoulder at the home position. In Fig. 4.2, we observe the force vectors of all the joints at the instant the right arm is at the final position i.e. outstretched so that the maze is in full view of the iCub. In both figures, the x axis is shown in red, the y axis is shown in green and the z axis is shown in blue.

An analysis of all the position vectors of the joints in Fig. 4.2 provides us proof that the calculation of the transformation matrices are accurate. It needs to be pointed out that, at this stage, the system is only in an initial stage. In order to solve the maze, the parameters of the joints need to be altered. This aspect of the problem would be taken care of by the core algorithm itself.

References

Breazeal, C., Wang, A., & Picard, R. (2007). Experiments with a Robotic Computer: Body, Affect and Cognition Interactions. *HRI'07* (pp. 153–160). Arlington, Virginia: ACM.

Forsyth, D., & Ponce. (2011). *Computer Vision: A Modern Approach.* Prentice Hall.

Harnad, S. (1995). *Grounding Symbolic Capacity in Robotic Capacity.* New Haven: Lawrence Erlbaum.

Kormushev, P., Calinon, S., Saegusa, R., & Metta, G. (2010). Learning the skill of archery by a humanoid iCub. *2010 IEEE-RAS International Conference on Humanoid Robotics.* Nashville.

Metta, G., Sandini, G., Vernon, D., & Natale, L. (2008). The iCub humanoid robot: an open platform for research in embodied cognition. *8th Workshop on performance metrics for intelligent systems.* ACM.

Nath, V., & Levinson, S. (2013a). Learning to Fire at Targets by an iCub Humanoid Robot. *AAAI Spring Symposium.* Palo Alto: AAAI.

Nath, V., & Levinson, S. (2013b). *Usage of computer vision and machine learning to solve 3D mazes.* Urbana: University of Illinois at Urbana-Champaign.

Nath, V., & Levinson, S. (2014). Solving 3D Mazes with Machine Learning: A prelude to deep learning using the iCub Humanoid Robot. *Twenty-Eighth AAAI Conference. Quebec City: AAAI*

Russell, S., & Norvig, P. (2010). *Artificial Intelligence, A Modern Approach.* New Jersey: Prentice Hall.

Sandini, G., Metta, G., & Vernon, G. (2007). The iCub Cognitive Humanoid Robot: An Open-System Research Platform for Enactive Cognition. *In 50 years of artificial intelligence* (pp. 358–369). Berlin Heidelburg: Springer Berlin Heidelberg.

Spong, M. W., Hutchinson, S., & Vidyasagar, M. (2006). *Robot Modelling and Control.* New Jersey: John Wiley & Sons.

Sutton, R. S., & Barto, A. G. (1998). *Reinforcement learning: An Introduction.* Cambridge: MIT Press.

Tsagarakis, N., Metta, G., & Vernon, D. (2007). iCUb: The design and realization of an open humanoid platform for cognitive and neuroscience research. *Advanced Robots 21.10,* (pp. 1151–1175).

Chapter 5
Computer Vision

Abstract In this chapter, we present the various components of the computer vision algorithms that were used for the various aspects of the project. Initially, the chapter discusses the underlying algorithms of computer vision from a mathematical standpoint. Once this aspect has been completed, the next step would be to demonstrate to the reader how we incorporated the algorithms to fir the specific problem that the research project intended to solve.

5.1 Inverse Homography

As part of the training process, every maze needs to be studied in order to develop a control policy. In an ideal scenario, a perfect orthographic view of the maze would be difficult to obtain at all times. This is especially true when the maze is tilted away from the robot along the axis of viewing. As a result, an inverse homography of the maze must be performed. In order to do so, identification of features with known geometric relationships to each other is the first step. At least four such features must be identified to determine the inverse homography of the maze. We felt that the easiest way to do this was to place high contrast color markers at the four corners of the maze board. The color red was used as the four color markers and we agreed not to use the color red anywhere else on the maze. The only other red colored object was the ball that was used to solve the maze.

All point coordinates on the maze are represented in a 2-dimensional form, i.e. as (x, y). However, in order for inverse homography to be performed, we require homogenous image coordinates.

The conversion of image coordinates to homogenous image coordinates is a fairly straightforward process and is shown by (5.1) below (Lazebnik 2013).

$$(x, y) => \begin{bmatrix} x \\ y \\ 1 \end{bmatrix} \tag{5.1}$$

Given the homogenous coordinate, the equation for homography is given below as (5.2) and (5.3) (Lazebnik 2013).

$$\lambda x_i' = H x_i \tag{5.2}$$

$$x_i' \times H x_i = 0 \tag{5.3}$$

Equations (5.2) and (5.3) can be expanded as follows:

$$\lambda \begin{bmatrix} x_i' \\ y_i' \\ 1 \end{bmatrix} = \begin{bmatrix} h_{11} & h_{12} & h_{13} \\ h_{21} & h_{22} & h_{23} \\ h_{31} & h_{32} & h_{33} \end{bmatrix} \begin{bmatrix} x_i \\ y_i \\ 1 \end{bmatrix} \tag{5.4}$$

$$\begin{bmatrix} x_i' \\ y_i' \\ 1 \end{bmatrix} \times \begin{bmatrix} h_1^T x_i \\ h_2^T x_i \\ h_3^T x_i \end{bmatrix} = \begin{bmatrix} y_i' h_3^T x_i - h_2^T x_i \\ h_1^T x_i - x_i' h_3^T x_i \\ x_i' h_2^T x_i - y_i' h_1^T x_i \end{bmatrix} \tag{5.5}$$

Equation (5.5) can re-written as (5.6) given below (Lazebnik 2013).

$$\begin{bmatrix} 0^T & -x_i^T & y_i' x_i^T \\ x_i^T & 0^T & -x_i' x_i^T \\ -y_i' x_i^T & x_i' x_i^T & 0^T \end{bmatrix} \begin{bmatrix} h_1 \\ h_2 \\ h_3 \end{bmatrix} = 0 \tag{5.6}$$

Equation (5.6) has three equations, of which only two are linearly independent. Furthermore, (5.6) is of the form

$$\mathbf{Ah = 0}$$

H can be determined by using homogenous least squares, i.e. by minimizing $\|Ah\|^2$. Figure 5.1 shows the abstraction of the maze with markers while Fig. 5.2 shows the unprojected coordinates of the maze after inverse homography.

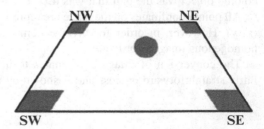

Fig. 5.1 Abstraction of maze with markers (Nath and Levinson 2014)

Fig. 5.2 Unprojected coordinates of the maze after inverse homography (Nath and Levinson 2014)

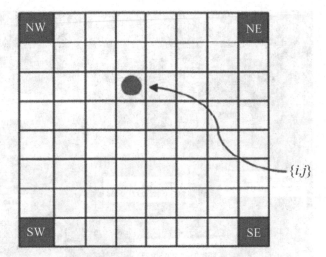

5.2 Offline Analysis of the Maze

At this stage, the inverse homography has been completed and an orthographic view of the maze board is expected at all times as visual input for the iCub. The next step would be to threshold the orthographic view to determine the layout of the maze. Thresholding by color would result in a binary image indicating the regions where a high concentration of red is present. In order to determine that this is indeed a good approach, we decided to determine the RGB values of various points in the image. The results are shown in Fig. 5.3.

Figure 5.3 is the image before any color correction or HSV mapping was applied. The unmapped RGB values are seen to have a very wide variation in value indicating that the raw RGB values are not good for thresholding. As a result, the approach to use RGB values to perform an image threshold was cancelled. The other approach was to use HSV mapping instead and this approach yielded much better results. For the sake of continuity, the results of the HSV mapping are examined in detail in Chap. 7. As a result, we decided to proceed with the HSV values instead.

A segmentation algorithm like RasterScan can be used to label contiguous regions and sort them by size (Buşoniu et al. 2010). In the processed image, the four largest regions are expected to be the four corner markers. The rest of the surrounding border content is cropped off in order to conserve the computational resources of the iCub, since video processing is a computationally intensive process. After the cropping has taken place, what is left are the maze walls and the open path. Once again, a RasterScan will provide the open contiguous path of the maze. Once a complete path is obtained, it can be discretized yet again into an n × n grid. Figure 5.4 shows the resultant image at this stage, after performing the second RasterScan operation.

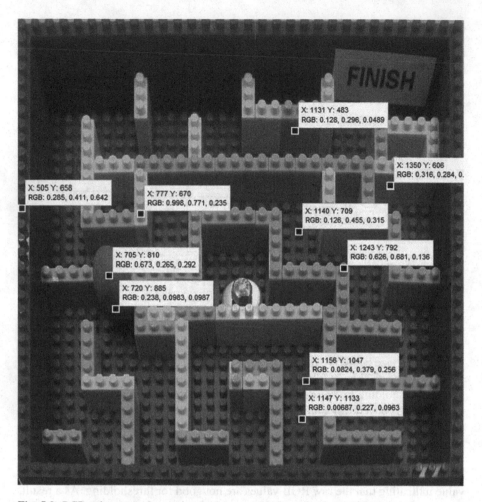

Fig. 5.3 RGB values at various points in the maze (Nath and Levinson 2014)

Another important thing that deserves mention is the start and end points of the maze. They need to be tagged so that the iCub can determine the start and end points. While it might seem like a trivial problem, it is actually quite hard to determine the two positions for extremely complicated mazes. As a result, the maze board itself contains two labels that have been manually placed on the board that denote the start and end points. Figure 5.5 shows how this seems to the resultant path that has been generated. Once a start and end point are associated with this path, reinforcement learning can begin. The reinforcement learning simulates trial and error runs of a simulated maze environment. The control actions involve course wrist motion with long pauses. After each action, the ball will come

Fig. 5.4 Resultant path
after Raster Scan applied
(Nath and Levinson 2014)

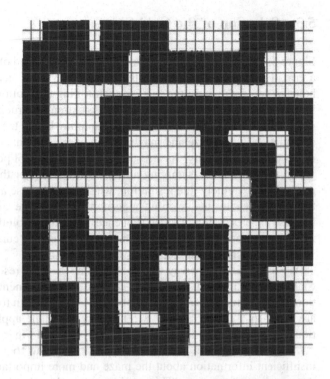

Fig. 5.5 Labelled start
and end points (Nath
and Levinson 2014)

to rest at one of the corners of the maze. After a sufficiently long run, time value
iteration converges and an optimal policy is obtained. Filtering of the optimal
policy provides more general control domains. The final filtered control policy
corresponding to the n × n is then saved for online control.

5.3   Selection of the Grid Size

Figure 5.4 shows the resultant path after the second round of RasterScan, along with a grid. The grid is necessary for the online analysis of any given maze because it helps to derive the optimum rules for controlling the motion of the ball, and can be localized on a regional basis. However, it is extremely crucial to determine the ideal resolution for sampling the video feed. Sampling below the video feed would cause degradation in the maze and may result in open segments of the maze, when there might be none in reality. As a result, the learned control policy is bound to fail.

On the other hand, sampling at a level much higher than the threshold would produce an extremely fine resolution, which would cause a tremendous increase in the time taken by the learning algorithm to converge upon a solution. This is because the processing of video sequences at a high resolution is a computationally intensive process. This issue is often referred to as the "curse of dimensionality" in various research literature (Forsyth and Ponce 2011).

We felt that the only way we can determine the ideal resolution would be using a trial-and-error method. In order to do this, we experimented with several resolutions and eventually narrowed the possible choices down to three resolutions. They are 16×16, 32×32 and 50×50. The result of the application of these resolutions on the maze and the resultant path is shown in Fig. 5.6 below respectively.

As can be seen from Fig. 5.6, the application of the 16×16 grid would result in insufficient information about the maze and more importantly, when the ball is at those regions of the maze. This would result in the robot behaving in a random and unexpected manner and is not a desirable action. Therefore, this resolution was also discarded from the pile of possible candidates. The next resolution that was tested was the 50×50 resolution. In this case, the robot would definitely be able to determine the location of the ball with respect to the maze. By visually observing the rightmost image of Fig. 5.6, it can easily be seen that the entire maze path is present and the granularity of the grid is extremely fine. Upon testing the robot to solve the maze using this resolution, it was determined that this results in

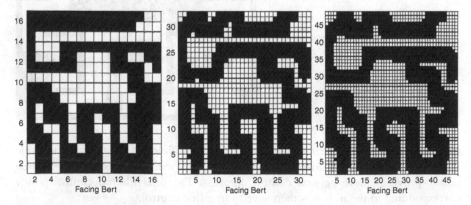

Fig. 5.6 Deciding on grid resolution from short listed options (Nath and Levinson 2014)

an unacceptably long time duration. The duration to constantly locate the ball with respect to its surroundings is very crucial since the maze solving has to take place online.

The last resolution that is left is the one of grid size 32×32. This resolution strikes a compromise between the two other resolutions. As can be visually seen from the middle image in Fig. 5.6, the 32×32 resolution would be able to determine the location of the ball with respect to the maze. For the purposes of this experiment, there is no anticipated loss of information by using this resolution. Upon testing the robot to solve the maze using the 32×32 resolution, it was determined that the robot was able to solve the maze online. As a result, it was decided to use a grid of size 32×32 to handle the video feed for online analysis.

5.4 Online Analysis

Once the optimal control policy has been obtained with the offline analysis of multiple mazes, as part of the training set, the iCub can solve any maze given to it. The test maze is vied from a projected perspective. Even in the online analysis of the maze, HSV color thresholding is performed so that a binary image indicating the high concentrations of red are obtained. This image shows the location of the ball and the four markers at the edge of the maze board. The iCub then applies the optimal control policy that has been learnt through all the training iterations that it went through. This would result in the iCub orienting the board along one of the three possible axes and wait for a period of time, to allow the ball to roll and stop at a corner, before levelling the board once again. The experimental run of the maze, being performed online, is examined in detail in Chap. 7.

References

Begum, M., & Karray, F. (2011). Visual Attention for Robotic Cognition: A Survey. *IEEE Transactions on Autonomous Mental Development*.

Buşoniu, L., Babuška, R., De Schutter, B., & Ernst, D. (2010). *Reinforcement Learning and Dynamic Programming Using Function Approximators*. CRC Press.

Forsyth, D., & Ponce. (2011). *Computer Vision: A Modern Approach*. Prentice Hall.

Harnad, S. (1995). *Grounding Symbolic Capacity in Robotic Capacity*. New Haven: Lawrence Erlbaum.

Kormushev, P., Calinon, S., Saegusa, R., & Metta, G. (2010). Learning the skill of archery by a humanoid iCub. *2010 IEEE-RAS International Conference on Humanoid Robotics*. Nashville.

Lazebnik, S. (2013). *Alignment* [PDF Document]. Retrieved from Lecture Notes Online Web site: http://www.cs.illinois.edu/~slazebni/spring13/lec12_alignment.pdf

Metta, G., Sandini, G., Vernon, D., & Natale, L. (2008). The iCub humanoid robot: an open platform for research in embodied cognition. *8th Workshop on performance metrics for intelligent systems*. ACM.

Michalski, Carbonell, & Mitchell, T. (1983). *Machine Learning*. Palo Alto: Tioga Publishing Company.

Nath, V., & Levinson, S. (2013a). Learning to Fire at Targets by an iCub Humanoid Robot. *AAAI Spring Symposium*. Palo Alto: AAAI.

Nath, V., & Levinson, S. (2013b). *Usage of computer vision and machine learning to solve 3D mazes*. Urbana: University of Illinois at Urbana-Champaign.

Nath, V., & Levinson, S. (2014). Solving 3D Mazes with Machine Learning: A prelude to deep learning using the iCub Humanoid Robot. *Twenty-Eighth AAAI Conference*. Quebec City: AAAI

Russell, S., & Norvig, P. (2010). *Artificial Intelligence, A Modern Approach*. New Jersey: Prentice Hall.

Sandini, G., Metta, G., & Vernon, G. (2007). The iCub Cognitive Humanoid Robot: An Open-System Research Platform for Enactive Cognition. *In 50 years of artificial intelligence* (pp. 358–369). Berlin Heidelberg: Springer Berlin Heidelberg.

Sigaud, O., & Buffet, O. (2010). *Markov Decision Processes in Artificial Intelligence*. Wiley.

Tsagarakis, N., Metta, G., & Vernon, D. (2007). iCUb: The design and realization of an open humanoid platform for cognitive and neuroscience research. *Advanced Robots 21.10*, (pp. 1151–1175).

Chapter 6
Machine Learning

Abstract Whenever a problem seems extremely open ended with a large variety of random variables that have an effect on the process, it is impossible for a human programmer to be able to account for every single case. The number of cases increases dramatically with an additional parameter. In such scenarios, probabilistic algorithms have the greatest applicability. The algorithms need to be given a couple of examples of scenarios it might come across and the algorithm would be able to handle a new scenario with reasonable accuracy. The key word in the previous statement is "reasonable". There is no probabilistic algorithm that will always return the optimum result with a probability of 1. That would make it a deterministic algorithm which, as has just been discussed, cannot handle every potential case. In this chapter, we discuss the algorithms that were employed to successfully complete the experiment.

6.1 Overview of Machine Learning

Machine learning can be broadly thought of as the programming of an algorithm to constantly improvise itself, based on available data. However, the type of learning to be used depends a lot on the type of data being dealt with, i.e. there isn't any one size fits all policy that can be run. It is important to remember that machine learning has a probabilistic approach, i.e. it might be possible to use ML techniques to come really close to solving a problem, but it would never be able to do the task with absolute certainty. If a graph were plotted on the accuracy of machine learning based algorithms, even the best algorithms would only asymptotically approach 100 %, but never quite get there. On the other hand, if the programmer is aware of all the possible scenarios and if it is humanely possible to address all of them, then the usual programming model is recommended, wherein each individual case/state is addressed. However, we find such simple scenarios are few in number, and that

V. Nath and S.E. Levinson, *Autonomous Robotics and Deep Learning*, SpringerBriefs   39
in Computer Science, DOI 10.1007/978-3-319-05603-6_6, © The Author(s) 2014

scenarios that model real life would have a vast number of variables that would be too complicated to model using a computer program. It is here that the programmer needs to use machine learning techniques in order to develop an approach that would return reasonably accurate solutions.

As previously mentioned, the type of learning algorithm to be used depends on the type of the data. If the data is unlabeled, i.e. if each row of data doesn't contain any associated label with it, the data is called unlabeled data. If the data is labeled, then the data is called labeled data. For example, the weather yesterday could be represented by the vector <1, 0, 1, 0, 1, 1, 1, 0>, where each digit represents a feature that is of interest. While the features have been represented, the data has not been labeled, i.e. whether this data represents a sunny or rainy or windy day. On the other hand, consider another vector <0, 1, 1, 1, 0, 0, 0, "snow"> contains a label that mentions that the data represents, which is also the desired output for any algorithm. In the former case, the data is called unlabeled data, while in the latter, the data is called labeled data.

In the case of unlabeled data, usually *clustering* takes place, i.e. elements or data points that are similar to each other tend to group together because of their common characteristics. When this takes place, the algorithm would be good at matching a new input to one of the existing clusters, although it would have no understanding whatsoever of what the data represents; the matching is based on how close the data seem to be with each clusters and then picks the closest one (Russell and Norvig 2010). Of course, it is possible for the algorithm to go wrong, and there would no way for the algorithm to detect that it was a mistake and take corrective action. This is why the training data is very important for unlabeled data. In such a case, when there is no feedback about the accuracy of the data, the type of learning is called *unsupervised learning* (Russell and Norvig 2010).

In the case of labeled data, the desired output is already present as part of the data itself. Therefore, it would be possible to determine a mapping function from the input to the output, based on the data provided. In this case, the algorithm would initially form a function based on the first few training examples it has seen. As it progresses through the training data, mistakes would be made and corrective action would be taken so that the mapping function can map from input to output in the best possible way. Once a function has been trained "enough", it should be able to accurately classify an unseen data point, from the test data. In reality, a function might not be able to get every single test data point accurately, and will have an error function associated with it. This method of learning is called *supervised learning* (Russell and Norvig 2010).

There is another type of learning which seems to resemble real life much closer than the previous two types of learning that has been discussed. In the case of *reinforcement learning*, the agent learns from reinforcements that are present in the data. The goal of the agent is to achieve the stated objective, which carries the highest reward (Russell and Norvig 2010). Paths that seem beneficial are assigned a positive reward score, while paths deemed detrimental are assigned a negative score.

The agent attempts to find the path with the highest overall reward, while trying to minimize the punishment/negative reward. An interesting thing is that the optimum path might contain negative paths, or lower positive rewards than other comparable intermediate paths. Yet, the agent would attempt to try for the overall highest reward. This is very similar to our day to day lives. For instance, a lot of children might not like going to school. To them, there is no immediate benefit in attending school. On the contrary, they might consider it a punishment. However, hardly anyone of us would argue about the value of education. In the long run, a person who went to school is more likely to do well than someone who did not go to school. Therefore, although it might seem like a negative reward, children need to attend school. Similarly, plenty of people eat healthy, avoid processed and unhealthy food and exercise regularly. In the immediate short term, indulging in processed food might seem better because of the pleasant taste. People who exercise regularly might not necessarily see its benefits right away. However, in the long term, taking care of one's body is very important and achieving this might seem wasting a lot of short term happiness. We also coined a phrase "looking at the big picture" to reflect this way of thinking. All this can be mathematically modelled as reinforcement learning, and is used a lot in this book as one of the preferred machine learning algorithms. The reinforcement learning algorithms being used in this book are Q-learning and SARSA, both of which are discussed in detail in Sect. 4.2.

As aforementioned, unsupervised learning primarily includes clustering because of the lack of any labels in the data. There are other methods that also employ unsupervised learning like hidden Markov models. A detailed discussion of these topics is beyond the scope of this book and is not discussed.

Supervised learning, on the other hand, creates a mapping function from input to output that is constantly being improvised by the labeled training data. Supervised learning has a lot of applications in classification and in regression applications. One of the simplest and most commonly used classifier is the *perceptron*, which is a binary linear classifier. The perceptron converts an input, x, to an output f(x) that is either 0 or 1, based on the threshold function (Russell and Norvig 2010). The perceptron can be trained online. A perceptron would contain a *weight vector*, **w**, which determines the weightage of the corresponding feature that it represents. Furthermore, the perceptron has a *threshold function* which is given by **Threshold** (**w.x**), where

$$\text{Threshold}\,(a) = 1 \text{ if } a \geq 1, \text{and } 0 \text{ otherwise}$$

Although the feature vector, **x**, cannot be changed, the weight vector certainly can and is dynamic in nature. As the perceptron iterates through training examples, the weight vectors converge to a solution, one that classifies the data in a linear fashion. The update equation of the weight vector is given by (6.1) below, which is also called the perceptron learning rule (Russell and Norvig 2010).

$$w_i \leftarrow w_i + \alpha(y - threshold(x)) \times x_i \tag{6.1}$$

Another common classifier that is based on supervised learning is the *support vector machine* (SVM). It is a non-parametric method, i.e. the SVM would have to retain all the training examples. However, in practice, they might retain only a small fraction of the number of examples. SVMs construct a *maximum margin separator*, which is a decision boundary with the largest possible distance to example points. As a result, the generalization process can take place well. Furthermore, what is of great importance of SVMs is the fact that SVMs can use a *kernel function* to project points to a *higher dimensional space* in order to make them linearly separable (Russell and Norvig 2010). This is a key difference from the perceptron which assumes that all the data points are linearly separable.

There are several other types of classifiers that are based on supervised learning. One of the other common ones are the neural networks. The neural networks are composed of nodes that are connected by links. A link from one node to the next is to propagate the activation from node 1 to node 2, and a weight w that is associated with the weightage given to that link. Each node's input is taken as the weighted sum of all its inputs. The output of the node is based on an *activation function* which could be a hard threshold or a logistic function. If it is a hard threshold, the node is called *perceptron* (discussed above) and if it is a logistic function, then the node is called *sigmoid perceptron* (Russell and Norvig 2010). Other types of classifiers include Naïve Bayes', decision trees, linear regression and logistic regression. A detailed discussion of these classifiers, as well as other machine learning concepts, is beyond the scope of this book. Interested readers are encouraged to read the books mentioned in the References section for detailed information about machine learning concepts.

6.2 Learning Algorithm

The most robust learning algorithm that is resilient to noise is the Q-learning algorithm, belonging to the category reinforcement learning (Russell and Norvig 2010). In order to apply the Q-learning algorithm, we set a penalty at the start and a penalty for the total time taken, with a reward at the goal state or making sure that the ball reaches the end position.

The update equation for temporal difference Q-learning is given by (6.2) below (Russell and Norvig 2010).

$$Q(s,a) \leftarrow Q(s,a) + \alpha\left(R(s) + \gamma max_{a'}Q\left(s',a'\right) - Q(s,a)\right) \tag{6.2}$$

where α is the learning rate and γ is the discount factor.

Upon closer examination of (6.2), we observe that Q-learning backs up the best Q-value from the state that was reached in the observed transition. In other words, Q-learning does not pay any attention to the actual policy being followed. Therefore, it is also called an off-policy algorithm and so it would not generate a policy that would maximize the probability of solving the maze (Russell and Norvig 2010). However, there is clearly a need to maximize this probability and an on-policy algorithm is required. The SARSA algorithm seemed like a good choice since it was very similar to the Q-learning algorithm, but was an on-policy algorithm. The update equation for SARSA is given by (6.3) below (Russell and Norvig 2010).

$$Q(s,a) \leftarrow Q(s,a) + \alpha\left(R(s) + \gamma\, Q\left(s',a'\right) - Q(s,a)\right) \qquad (6.3)$$

While the difference between (6.2) and (6.3) may seem very subtle at first, there is a pretty significant difference between Q-learning and the SARSA algorithm. The SARSA algorithm actually waits until an action is taken and then updates the Q-value for that action. Simply put, if a greedy agent that always takes the action with the best Q-value is required, Q-learning is the algorithm to use. However, if exploration of the state space is required, SARSA is the algorithm that offers a lot more advantages. For the purposes of this experiment, an exploratory algorithm is required to maximize the probability of solving the maze correctly in the shortest time possible. The optimum policy for the SARSA is given by (6.4) below (Russell and Norvig 2010).

$$\pi^* = argmax_\pi \sum\nolimits_h P(h|e)u_h^\pi \qquad (6.4)$$

In (6.4), the posterior probability P(h|e) is obtained by using the Bayes' rule and applying it to the observations that have been obtained.

The learning for this experiment was done with value iterations of a discrete state-action space. The algorithm used a sample based quality space (Sutton and Barto 1998). The specific algorithm used is from (Buşoniu et al. 2010) and is given below. Here, φ is an index of discretized space and θ is the value at that index. The control space is $U = \{0, 1, 2, 3, 4\}$, where 0 is a random action and $\{1, 2, 3, 4\}$ is a wrist tilt in the direction {North East, North West, South West, South East} respectively.

The state space corresponds to the location in the 32×32 discretized path space of the maze. The value of α and γ were set to 0.99 and an exploration function of $\varepsilon = Q_{visist}^{-0.01}$ was used.

The pseudo-code of the algorithm is given below.

Q-Learning with Algorithm2.3:

\\---

Input: discount factor γ,

   exploration schedule $\{\epsilon_k\}_{k=0}^{\infty}$ s.t. $\sum_{k=0}^{\infty} \epsilon_k = \infty$,

   learning rate schedule $\{\alpha_k\}_{k=0}^{\infty} \in [0,1]$

   BFs $\phi_{[j]}: X \times U \rightarrow \mathbb{R}^{p(j)}$,

Initialize parameter vector, e.g., $\theta_0 \leftarrow 0$

Measure initial state x_0

For every time step $k = 0,1,2,\dots$ **do**

o $u_k \leftarrow \begin{cases} u \in \arg\max_{u'} \phi^T(x_k, u')\theta_\ell & P = 1 - \epsilon_k \\ \text{random action in } U & P = \epsilon_k \end{cases}$

o   Apply u_k, measure next state x_{k+1} and reward r_{k+1}

o $\theta_{\ell+1} \leftarrow \theta_\ell + \alpha_k [r_{k+1} + \gamma \max_{u'} \phi^T(x_{k+1}, u')\theta_\ell - \phi^T(x_k, u_k)\theta_\ell]\phi(x_k, u_k)$

end

\\---

References

Barber, D. (2012). *Bayesian Reasoning and Machine Learning*. Cambridge: University Press.

Breazeal, C., Wang, A., & Picard, R. (2007). Experiments with a Robotic Computer: Body, Affect and Cognition Interactions. *HRI' 07* (pp. 153–160). Arlington, Virginia: ACM.

Buşoniu, L., Babuška, R., De Schutter, B., & Ernst, D. (2010). *Reinforcement Learning and Dynamic Programming Using Function Approximators*. CRC Press.

Harnad, S. (1995). *Grounding Symbolic Capacity in Robotic Capacity*. New Haven: Lawrence Erlbaum.

Kormushev, P., Calinon, S., Saegusa, R., & Metta, G. (2010). Learning the skill of archery by a humanoid iCub. *2010 IEEE-RAS International Conference on Humanoid Robotics*. Nashville.

Metta, G., Sandini, G., Vernon, D., & Natale, L. (2008). The iCub humanoid robot: an open platform for research in embodied cognition. *8th Workshop on performance metrics for intelligent systems*. ACM.

Michalski, Carbonell, & Mitchell, T. (1983). *Machine Learning*. Palo Alto: Tioga Publishing Company.

Michie, D. (1986). *On Machine Intelligence*. New York: John Wiley & Sons.

Nath, V., & Levinson, S. (2013a). Learning to Fire at Targets by an iCub Humanoid Robot. *AAAI Spring Symposium*. Palo Alto: AAAI.

Nath, V., & Levinson, S. (2013b). *Usage of computer vision and machine learning to solve 3D mazes*. Urbana: University of Illinois at Urbana-Champaign.

Nath, V., & Levinson, S. (2014). Solving 3D Mazes with Machine Learning: A prelude to deep learning using the iCub Humanoid Robot. *Twenty-Eighth AAAI Conference. Quebec City: AAAI*

Russell, S., & Norvig, P. (2010). *Artificial Intelligence, A Modern Approach*. New Jersey: Prentice Hall.

Sandini, G., Metta, G., & Vernon, G. (2007). The iCub Cognitive Humanoid Robot: An Open-System Research Platform for Enactive Cognition. *In 50 years of artificial intelligence* (pp. 358–369). Berlin Heidelburg: Springer Berlin Heidelberg.

Sigaud, O., & Buffet, O. (2010). *Markov Decision Processes in Artificial Intelligence*. Wiley.

Sutton, R. S., & Barto, A. G. (1998). *Reinforcement learning: An Introduction*. Cambridge: MIT Press.

Tsagarakis, N., Metta, G., & Vernon, D. (2007). iCUb: The design and realization of an open humanoid platform for cognitive and neuroscience research. *Advanced Robots 21.10*, (pp. 1151–1175).

Chapter 7
Experimental Results

Abstract In this chapter, we discuss the results that were obtained while trying to solve an unknown maze by the iCub using the algorithm discussed in Chap. 6.

7.1 Open Loop Test

The first test performed was to test the hardware capability of the iCub, along with the durability of the maze board and the ability of the iCub to navigate the ball through all possible corners. In order to prove this, we programmed the iCub to solve a particular maze in an open loop i.e. the robot was pre-programmed to solve a maze of a particular arrangement. This first step allowed us to explore the basic command interface for the task, as well as address issues surrounding grasping and the field of view of the entire maze. The successful execution of this task would result in greater for the entire experiment. Figures 7.1 and 7.2 show the iCub working through the maze in this open loop test.

The iCub managed to complete the entire maze, from start to finish, successfully. The successful completion of the open loop test gave us great confidence that the iCub would be able to learn an optimum control policy and solve any given maze to it.

7.2 Closed Loop Test

Now that the open loop test was successfully completed, the next step was to perform a closed loop test on a maze that the robot has never seen before. However, it is imperative that the optimum control policy has been obtained by the learning algorithm employed by the iCub. Therefore, we trained the iCub on 23 different

V. Nath and S.E. Levinson, *Autonomous Robotics and Deep Learning*, SpringerBriefs in Computer Science, DOI 10.1007/978-3-319-05603-6_7, © The Author(s) 2014

Fig. 7.1 The iCub while
working through the open
loop test

Fig. 7.2 Next action
of the iCub while
working through
the open loop test

Fig. 7.3 Detection of the corners of the maze (Nath and Levinson 2014)

Fig. 7.4 Resultant Inverse Homography (Nath and Levinson 2014)

mazes, as part of the training set. Once this was done, we tested the iCub on 11 different mazes. The iCub successfully solved every single maze configuration, giving it an accuracy of 100 %. This section will walk you through all the parts of the experiment while solving a particular test maze.

The first step is to identify the corners of the maze board and then perform an inverse homography on the resulting image feed. Figures 7.3 shows the successful detection of the corners while Fig. 7.4 shows the resultant inverse homography.

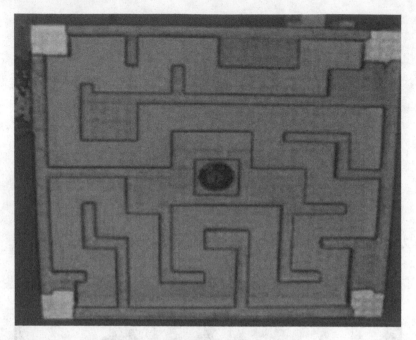

Fig. 7.5 Maze after HSV application (Nath and Levinson 2014)

Once the inverse homography has been obtained, the next step is to apply the HSV mapping to facilitate the detection of the features of the maze. Figure 7.5 shows the resultant HSV mapping applied to a particular maze configuration.

The RGB image of the maze that resulted from inverse homography after the application of the 32×32 grid is shown in Fig. 7.6.

The path that resulted from the application of Raster Scan and the labelling of the start and end points have already been shown as Figs. 5.4 and 5.5 respectively. Once this point is done, reinforcement learning is performed on the resultant maze with a penalty at the start, a reward at the goal and a running time penalty. This results in a motivation for the algorithm to determine a path from the start to the end point in optimal time. The value function of this approach is shown in Fig. 7.7 below.

The optimal control policy is then computed from the quality space. For control values that have the same numerical value, one of them is chosen at random. The resulting control policy is shown in Fig. 7.8 below.

As can be seen from Fig. 7.8, the control policy is scattered across various neighboring points. This would result in an unstable motion of the robot's hand while solving the maze, making it susceptible to increased hardware wear and tear. A filter can then be applied to the control policy to obtain a smoothed out policy for the maze. The resultant optimal control policy for the maze is shown in Fig. 7.9 below. It is this output that is being used for the online maze solving by the iCub robot.

Fig. 7.6 RGB version of
the maze after inverse
homography and grid
application

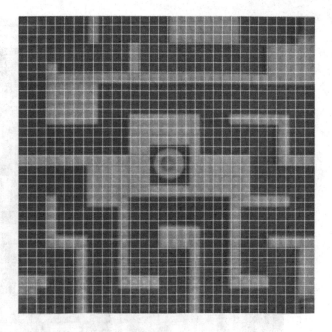

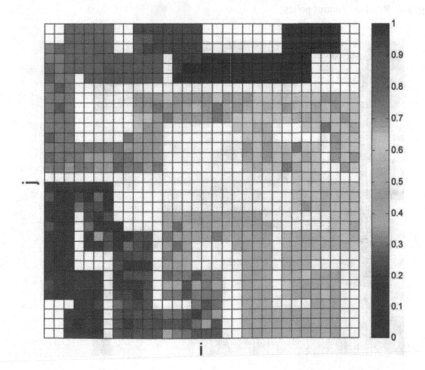

Fig. 7.7 Normalized log value function for the maze

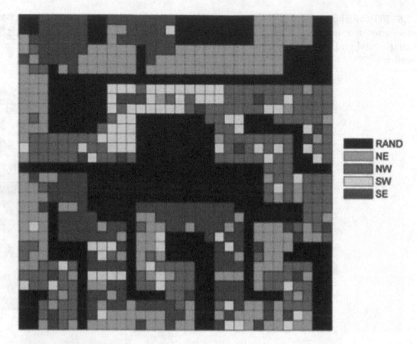

Fig. 7.8 Resultant control policy

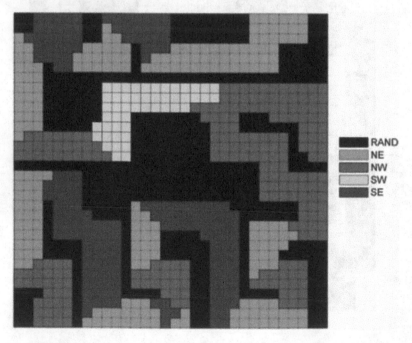

Fig. 7.9 Optimal control policy after smoothing

The following set of figures show the entire actual sequence of solving this particular maze as seen from the iCub's right eye, in RGB view. Each sequence consists of the current maze in RGB form, the Raster Scan visualization of the position of the ball with respect to the four corners, and lastly the position of the ball in the maze with respect to the grid with the next direction to be applied indicated by the arrow inside the circle.

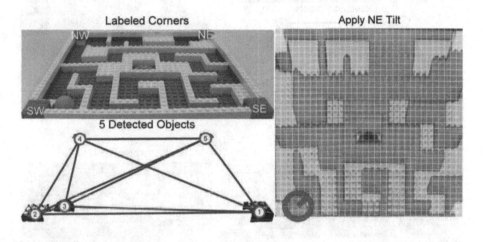

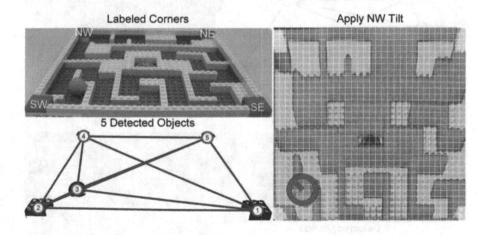

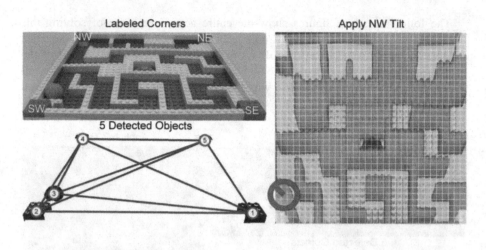

Labeled Corners — Apply NW Tilt

5 Detected Objects

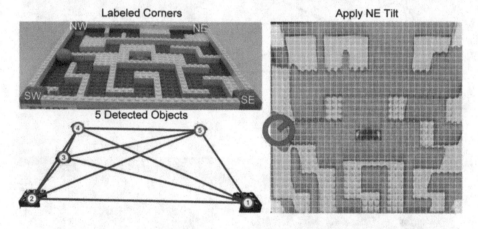

Labeled Corners — Apply NE Tilt

5 Detected Objects

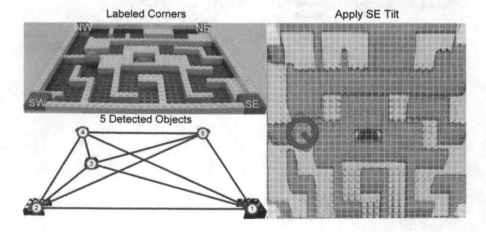

Labeled Corners — Apply SE Tilt

5 Detected Objects

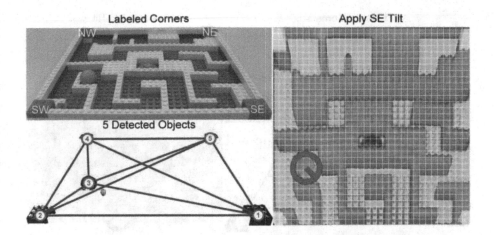

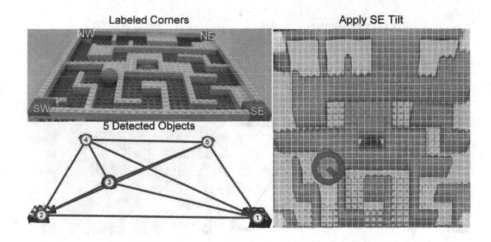

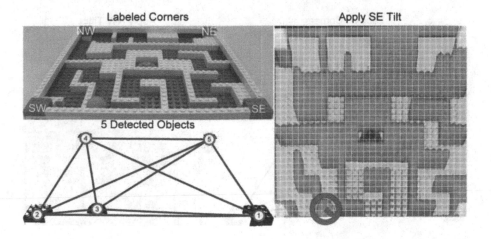

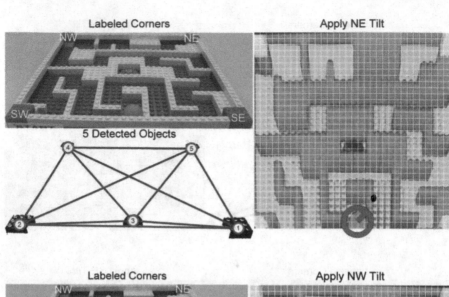

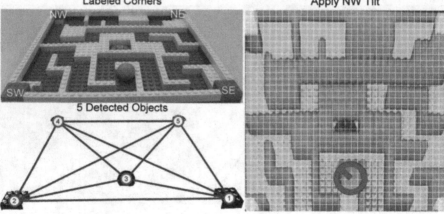

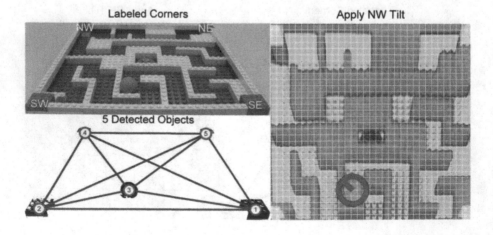

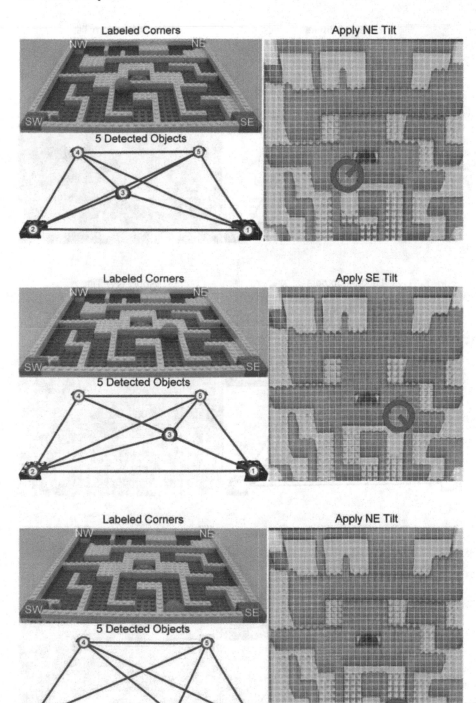

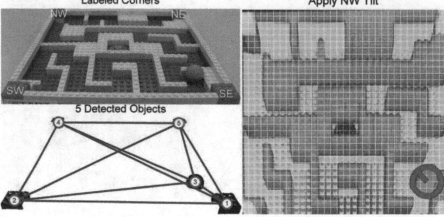

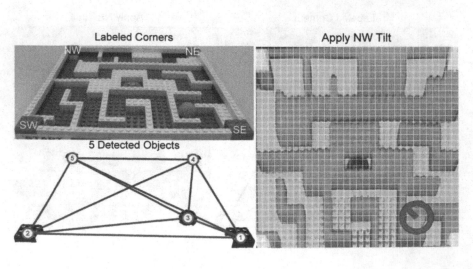

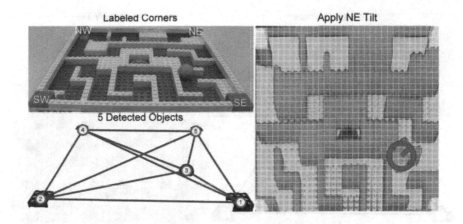

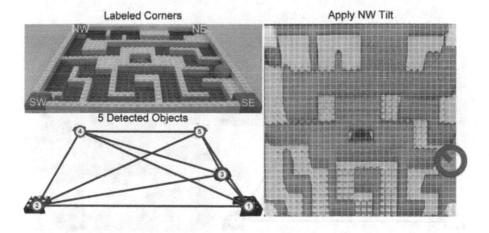

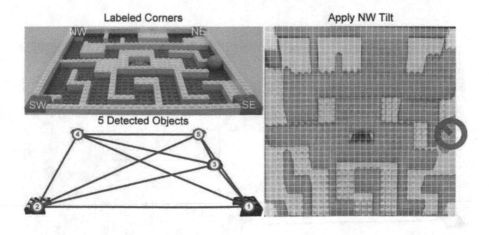

Labeled Corners

Apply NW Tilt

5 Detected Objects

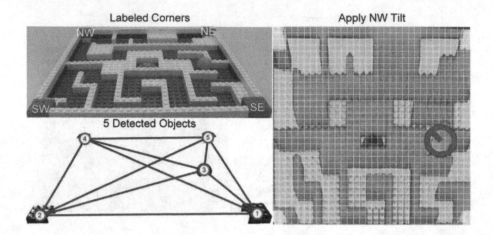

Labeled Corners

Apply NW Tilt

5 Detected Objects

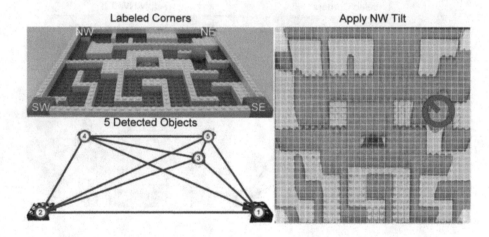

Labeled Corners

Apply SW Tilt

5 Detected Objects

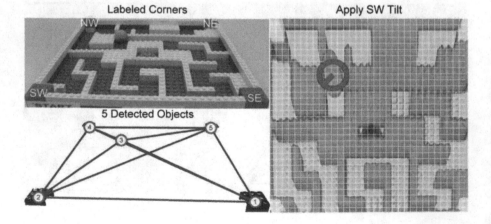

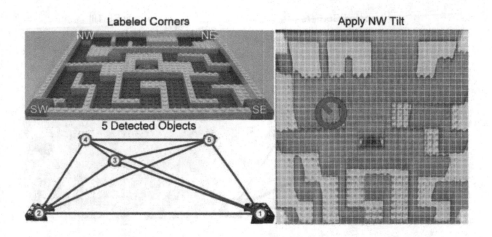

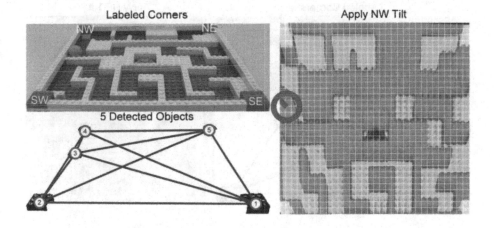

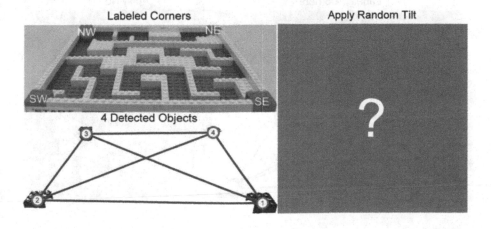

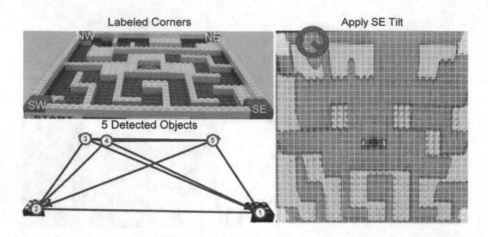

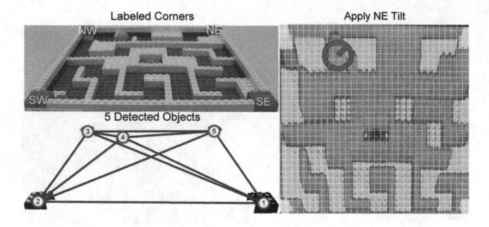

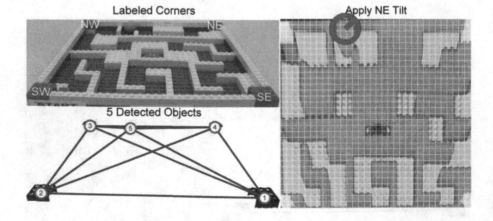

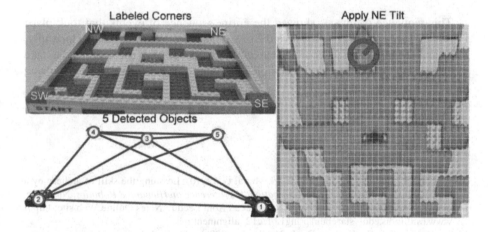

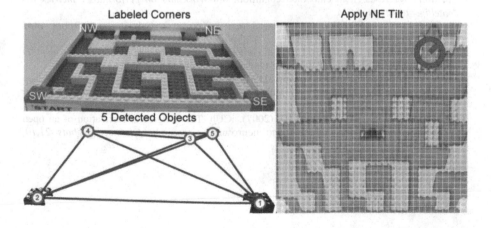

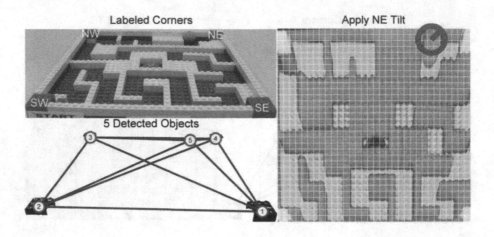

This sequence of images showed the entire sequence of events that took place from the iCub's perspective to solve the given maze from start to finish. Hopefully, this sequence gave the reader an idea about the sequence of events that need to take place in order to accomplish the complete solving of a 3-dimensional maze using machine learning.

References

Kormushev, P., Calinon, S., Saegusa, R., & Metta, G. (2010). Learning the skill of archery by a humanoid iCub. *2010 IEEE-RAS International Conference on Humanoid Robotics*. Nashville.

Lazebnik, S. *Alignment* [PDF Document]. Retrieved from Lecture Notes Online Web site: http://www.cs.illinois.edu/~slazebni/spring13/lec12_alignment.pdf

Metta, G., Sandini, G., Vernon, D., & Natale, L. (2008). The iCub humanoid robot: an open platform for research in embodied cognition. *8th Workshop on performance metrics for intelligent systems*. ACM.

Nath, V., & Levinson, S. (2013a). Learning to Fire at Targets by an iCub Humanoid Robot. *AAAI Spring Symposium*. Palo Alto: AAAI.

Nath, V., & Levinson, S. (2013b). *Usage of computer vision and machine learning to solve 3D mazes*. Urbana: University of Illinois at Urbana-Champaign.

Nath, V., & Levinson, S. (2014). Solving 3D Mazes with Machine Learning: A prelude to deep learning using the iCub Humanoid Robot. *Twenty-Eighth AAAI Conference. Quebec City: AAAI*

Tsagarakis, N., Metta, G., & Vernon, D. (2007). iCUb: The design and realization of an open humanoid platform for cognitive and neuroscience research. *Advanced Robots 21.10*, (pp. 1151–1175).

Chapter 8
Future Direction

A simple literature review will reveal a plethora of maze solving algorithms. However, merely executing an algorithm in a sequence of steps is not worthy of present day research, simply because there is nothing to differentiate it from the millions of sequential executions taking place in an ordinary CPU. Furthermore, if the system finds itself in an unknown state, most algorithms do not have a fallback mechanism built into the algorithm. Engineers will have to add some sort of safety check just to get the system back to a known condition. There are times when even this is not sufficient since the exact sequence of states and timing is crucial for the successful termination of the algorithm.

In this book, we have presented a unique way to solve any given 3-dimensional maze. The method is unique because of the learning component that has been added into the process, making it a truly generic algorithm that is resilient to environmental changes and landing in unexpected states. Of critical research importance is the understanding of the evolving model that the iCub is formulating as it keeps going through the training examples and sees more test cases. It is also very interesting to understand how the iCub, or any intelligent agent for that matter, applies the model to solve a problem it hasn't seen before. This understanding is crucial because it takes us one step closer to attaining strong AI, wherein robots can "realize" that they are agents that have the potential to influence and alter the environment around them through actions that they perform. This approach is very similar to the cognitive development of human infants. Initially, they simply wave their arms and legs randomly. This is very similar to the approach of motor babbling in the domain of robotics, wherein a robot would be able to autonomously develop an internal model of its own body and its immediate environment. In the case of the human infant, as it ages, more neuron connections are being made in its brain. Soon enough, the infant is able to make a connection that by shaking the rattle in its hand, it can produce some noise. In purely technical terms, a feedback loop has just been completed.

We believe that the iCub platform and the community of AI researchers are currently at this stage. The iCub has "realized" that by altering the orientation of the board, it can cause the ball to roll in a particular direction. Figure 7.9 in Sect. 7.2

V. Nath and S.E. Levinson, *Autonomous Robotics and Deep Learning*, SpringerBriefs in Computer Science, DOI 10.1007/978-3-319-05603-6_8, © The Author(s) 2014

shows the regions of the maze after the optimum control policy has been smoothed out. All that the iCub needs to do at this point is to ensure that the generated optimum control policy is being followed. If not, corrective action would be taken also based on the control policy. In a way, this approach can be considered to be a Mealy state machine, with each action changing the state and bringing the system to a new state. This happens in an iterative manner, just like traversing a state machine is. Therefore, while strong AI has definitely not been attained so far, we believe that fringing the boundary has begun to occur, at least in terms of observable behavior. While we aren't there yet, we believe that strong AI is indeed a possibility, at least in terms of observable behavior that rivals that of an average human. Hopefully, the goal of developing a truly conscious entity will become a reality very soon.

References

Asimov, I. (2008). *I, Robot*. Spectra.

Harnad, S. (1995). *Grounding Symbolic Capacity in Robotic Capacity*. New Haven: Lawrence Erlbaum.

Kormushev, P., Calinon, S., Saegusa, R., & Metta, G. (2010). Learning the skill of archery by a humanoid iCub. *2010 IEEE-RAS International Conference on Humanoid Robotics*. Nashville.

Metta, G., Sandini, G., Vernon, D., & Natale, L. (2008). The iCub humanoid robot: an open platform for research in embodied cognition. *8th Workshop on performance metrics for intelligent systems*. ACM.

Michie, D. (1986). *On Machine Intelligence*. New York: John Wiley & Sons.

Nath, V., & Levinson, S. (2013a). Learning to Fire at Targets by an iCub Humanoid Robot. *AAAI Spring Symposium*. Palo Alto: AAAI.

Nath, V., & Levinson, S. (2013b). *Usage of computer vision and machine learning to solve 3D mazes*. Urbana: University of Illinois at Urbana-Champaign.

Nath, V., & Levinson, S. (2014). Solving 3D Mazes with Machine Learning: A prelude to deep learning using the iCub Humanoid Robot. *Twenty-Eighth AAAI Conference*. Quebec City: AAAI.

Russell, S., & Norvig, P. (2010). *Artificial Intelligence, A Modern Approach*. New Jersey: Prentice Hall.

Sandini, G., Metta, G., & Vernon, G. (2007). The iCub Cognitive Humanoid Robot: An Open-System Research Platform for Enactive Cognition. *In 50 years of artificial intelligence* (pp. 358–369). Berlin Heidelburg: Springer Berlin Heidelberg.

Spong, M. W., Hutchinson, S., & Vidyasagar, M. (2006). *Robot Modelling and Control*. New Jersey: John Wiley & Sons.

Tsagarakis, N., Metta, G., & Vernon, D. (2007). iCUb: The design and realization of an open humanoid platform for cognitive and neuroscience research. *Advanced Robots 21.10*, (pp. 1151-1175).

Wells, H. (2005). *The War of the Worlds*. New York: NYRB Classics.